DARKNESS
VISIBLE

PHILIP PULLMAN
AND *HIS DARK MATERIALS*

NICHOLAS TUCKER

ICON

First published in the UK in 2003 by Wizard Books,
an imprint of Icon Books, Omnibus Business Centre,
39–41 North Road, London N7 9DP
email: info@iconbooks.com
www.iconbooks.com

This edition published in the UK in 2017 by Icon Books Ltd

Sold in the UK, Europe and Asia
by Faber & Faber Ltd, Bloomsbury House,
74–77 Great Russell Street,
London WC1B 3DA or their agents

Distributed in the UK, Europe and Asia
by Grantham Book Services,
Trent Road, Grantham NG31 7XQ

Distributed in Australia and New Zealand
by Allen & Unwin Pty Ltd,
PO Box 8500, 83 Alexander Street,
Crows Nest, NSW 2065

Distributed in South Africa
by Jonathan Ball, Office B4, The District,
41 Sir Lowry Road, Woodstock 7925

Distributed in India by Penguin Books India,
7th Floor, Infinity Tower – C, DLF Cyber City,
Gurgaon 122002, Haryana

Distributed in Canada by Publishers Group Canada,
76 Stafford Street, Unit 300, Toronto, Ontario M6J 2S1

Distributed in the USA by Publishers Group West,
1700 Fourth Street, Berkeley, CA 94710

ISBN: 978-1-78578-228-2

Typeset by Marie Doherty

Printed and bound in the UK by Clays Ltd, St Ives plc

DARKNESS
VISIBLE

To Thomas, Billy, Joseph, Mimi, Lydia,
Archie, Harry and Francis, with love.

ABOUT THE AUTHOR

Nicholas Tucker was first a teacher and then an educational psychologist before becoming Senior Lecturer in Cultural and Community Studies at the University of Sussex. A frequent reviewer and broadcaster, he has written many books on children and what they read.

ACKNOWLEDGEMENTS

I would like to thank Philip Pullman for his generous help, which made writing and then revising this book so much easier as well as more satisfying. Also a big thank you to Kim Reynolds as always, for her unfailing and ceaselessly stimulating interest and support. Kate Agnew was a marvellous editor, coming up with a whole series of excellent suggestions. Students I have taught at Sussex University and at the Roehampton Institute have also helped me greatly over the years, as have my own children and now grandchildren in all matters to do with children's literature.

CONTENTS

ILLUSTRATIONS

Philip Pullman

P hilip Pullman was born in Norwich in 1946, the son of an RAF fighter pilot. Moving around from station to station with his younger brother Francis, they settled for a time in what was then Southern Rhodesia. Returning to Britain in 1954, they heard that their father had died in a plane crash during a raid made against the rebel Mau Mau movement in Kenya. Neither son knew their father at all well, since he was so often away from home. He was awarded the Distinguished Flying Cross after his death, and there are newspaper pictures of Philip, then aged seven, standing with Francis outside Buckingham Palace just after his mother had received the medal on behalf of her late husband.

Years later, while going through some family papers, Pullman discovered that his mother and father were planning to divorce at the time of his father's death. This was a considerable shock, given that any hint of this family secret had previously been kept from him. As he wrote later, his father had for him always been 'a hero, steeped in glamour, killed in action defending his country'. But this image too became harder to sustain given the report of the details of the death which appeared in the *London Gazette* in 1954 and is worth quoting here in full:

> F/L.A.O Pullman was posted to Kenya on March 31st, 1953, in No.1340 Flight of Harvards, for operations against Mau Mau. The main task of the Harvards has been bombing and machine-gunning Mau Mau and their hideouts in the densely wooded and difficult country of the Aberdare Range and Mount Kenya. Pullman frequently carried out attacks which necessitated diving steeply into the gorges of Mathioya, Chania, Gura and Zuti rivers, and often in conditions of low cloud and driving rain. The citation says that he consistently displayed a fine offensive spirit and great determination in pressing home his attacks. He carried out a total of 3,400 hours flying, during which he completed 220 bombing and strafing sorties.

In 2008 the journalist Cole Moreton, in an interview with Pullman for the *Independent* newspaper, put it to him that despite these testing conditions there could hardly have been much opposition from the enemy at the time, given that the Mau Mau would have been unable to return any sort of effective fire. Reacting to what was to him new information, Pullman replied that: 'My father probably doesn't come out of this with very much credit, judged by the standards of modern liberal progressive thought.' Subsequent revelations

Wednesday   EASTER

FROM DRAYTON TO THE PALACE

*T*WO Drayton boys—
Francis and Philip
Pullman, aged five and
eight—went with their
mother, Mrs. Audrey
Pullman, to Bucking
ham Palace yesterday.
The picture shows
them after Mrs. Pull
man had received from
the Queen the Distin-
guished Flying Cross
conferred on her hus-
band, the late Flight
Lieut. Alfred Pullman.
R.A.F., for gallantry in
operations against the
Mau Mau in Kenya.
Aged 38, he was killed
in February.

Mrs. Pullman was re
ceived by the Queen in
a private room at the
Palace. Afterwards Mrs
Pullman said: "The
Queen shook hands
with both my boys and
asked me how long my
husband had been in
the Air Force, and how
old my sons were."

Mrs. Pullman said
her husband's D.F.C
was the first medal
awarded during the
Kenya operations.

'Huma
when
recorde

" Human fallib
official statement
for a baby girl
Hospital, Maccles
recorded as a boy
The mother M
Wilmslow (Ches
was told, 'It's a
round from the
child was later
Jeffrey James.

After an invest
today, the secreta
and District H
Committee issued
ment:—

"We are quite
is no possible
the babies.
births in the
one at 7.20 in
and the other
5.15 in the ever

"That also wa
fortunately, thro
on the part of
wife, was recor

A report of the
sent to the Mini
Mrs. Cooper c
when she foun
and not a boy

Weakness found in
Hannisburgh cliffs

T' URGES R.D.C

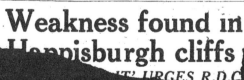

1. Article from the *Eastern Evening News*, 3 November 1954.
(Reprinted courtesy of the *Eastern Evening News*, Norwich.)

about sustained British civil and military brutality in Kenya during this time and after have further cemented this opinion.

The brave astronaut Lee Scoresby, who plays such a heroic part in *His Dark Materials*, was later chosen by Pullman, when talking to child readers, as his favourite character. Could he have been partly inspired by the young Pullman's idealisation of his father, a character created long before he was forced to admit to Cole Moreton that this new information he was now hearing amounted to 'a serious challenge to my childhood memory'?

It is not surprising therefore that Pullman often creates young characters in his fiction who have problems with their parents, sometimes stretching far back into the past. Dead or missing fathers are also a constant occurrence in his stories, and Pullman himself remembers that he was 'preoccupied for a long time by the mystery of what [his father] must have been like'. That mystery continues to the present day, in the sense that Pullman still feels certain that there was something not quite right about the reasons given for his father's fatal accident, put down to machine dysfunction. But his efforts to find out more have so far proved unsuccessful.

Returning to Britain, the two boys stayed in a Norfolk rectory with their mother's Welsh parents while she worked full time in London. Pullman's grandfather was an Anglican clergyman, who used to tell the boys a range of stories from sources that included the Bible, as well as tales he had heard in his role as occasional prison chaplain at Norwich Gaol.

2. Philip on right, aged about seven. (Reproduced by kind permission of Philip Pullman.)

One of his jobs was to accompany prisoners to the gallows after they had been condemned to death. With money always tight, he took up this additional duty as a matter of course. The boys were never aware of any extra strain involved, since their grandfather did not wish to upset them by letting them know the reason for these occasional absences. It was only years later, when Pullman was an adult, that his grandfather told him of the pain that this part of his job had caused him.

Far from turning him against religion, Pullman now remembers his grandfather as 'a wonderful man: gentle and humane as well as a marvellous storyteller'. He has also described him as 'the most important influence in my life'. Very much a traditional head of the household, and a gratifyingly important figure in the village, the boys' grandfather could be playful too. Above all, he was a man 'in whose presence you *wanted* to be good'. Pullman still loves the traditional language and atmospheric settings of the Bible and the Book of Common Prayer, so associated in his own mind with his grandfather. Regular visits to church and Sunday school occurred during this time. Years later, Pullman makes use of Biblical stories and imagery throughout *His Dark Materials*, even though his feelings have now turned against the Christian religion that he no longer believes in.

There was never enough room in his mother's small London flat for her children, nor could she afford to give up full-time work. But a child's fantasies are not concerned with objective reality. So it's also possible that some of the hostility felt for that ambiguous mother Mrs Coulter in *His Dark Materials* dates back to the small boy's anger and bewilderment at having been, in his eyes, temporarily abandoned by his own mother. Mrs Coulter, after all, combines both strongly positive and utterly negative images of womanhood. Could this contradictory mixture also reflect some of the conflicting feelings Philip may occasionally have felt towards his mother at the time? Now no longer alive, does she continue to live on in a number of her son's best works?

Pullman has, however, stated that Mrs Coulter is easily his favourite character after her daughter Lyra. Beautiful, wicked, unpredictable and amoral, her presence is always exciting. Absent mothers often attract all sorts of fantasies in the imagination of the children they leave behind, not all of them by any means negative. Mrs Coulter's undeniable charm and feminine allure, for example, are at one with the fantasies the young Philip had about his mother's supposedly fast-paced and glamorous city life away from her country-based family. Visiting her in London he remembers admiring her general sense of style, so different from the simplicities of rural Norfolk. There were also exciting theatre visits, and encounters with her various hard-drinking friends.

In conversation now he insists that at the time he took her absence for granted. He believes there was never any suffering on his part simply because his grandparents were providing all the love he and his brother needed. Living in a large rectory, the boys had plenty of room to play, constantly diving into their grandfather's extensive dressing-up collection, so often put to use in the various village pageants and processions he liked to organise. There was also a large garden and the run of the village at a time when traffic was minimal. But the prolonged absences of a mother, however good the reason, must still at times have been painful for a growing child.

His equally loving grandmother is remembered by Philip as constantly warm and gracious, as well as sharply intelligent. Her sister lived in the household too, a maiden lady who had been disappointed in love and had since become, in Pullman's own words, 'a bit of a drudge'. Somewhat frail and also totally devoted to the boys in a way that Pullman has described as simple-hearted in the purest sense, she made up the trio of older adults who provided the two children with an atmosphere of unconditional love.

Aged eight, Pullman attended a prep school near Norwich. It was there that a kindly teacher read him and fourteen other boys the whole of Coleridge's famous poem *The Rime of the Ancient Mariner*. Listening spellbound, Pullman felt gripped as never before, and began to wonder about one day becoming a writer himself. By now a stepfather had come along, also an RAF pilot, and the new family travelled halfway round the world in an ocean liner to a posting in Australia. In time Pullman was also to make long boat journeys to the Suez Canal, Bombay, Aden, Colombo, Las Palmas and Madeira as part of the restless life of any child whose father or stepfather was in one of the armed services.

3. A school photo of Philip at eight years.
(Reproduced by kind permission of Philip Pullman.)

It was on this particular voyage to Australia that the two boys, when both came down with scarlet fever, started inventing games as fierce as they were intense. Using a plastic construction kit to build forts and castles, they played out various imaginary conflicts for days at a time, each boy taking the part of either the good or bad guy as the situation demanded. Once they were settled into their new home, such games then became influenced by the Superman- and Batman-style comics, which the nine-year-old Philip totally adored.

There was also Australian radio, with its serials about Superman, cowboys and a kangaroo that kept tools in its pouch. With these this remarkable animal could repair almost anything, including broken-down trains, so on occasions saving valuable lives. Pullman now believes that it was the adventures of this kangaroo that kick-started his career as a storyteller. Each night, when the boys had gone to bed in their shared room and the light was turned off, Philip would sing out his version of the heroic kangaroo's radio signature tune. There would then follow a story made up on the spot, with neither Philip nor his brother Francis having any idea how it would end.

Pullman can still recall the feeling of excitement as each story seemed to find its own particular path, just as his stories do today, often to the surprise of the author himself. That section of the National Curriculum that requires all pupils in schools today to make a plan before writing their own story is particularly detested by Pullman. For him, this is the equivalent to killing off the imagination before it has even had a chance to get started.

The following year Philip, now aged ten, was back in Britain, first at a prep school in Battersea and then at Ysgol Ardudwy, a state school in Harlech: the last of the eight different schools he was to attend. This coincided with a move by the family to Wales, with Pullman's stepfather resigning as an RAF pilot to concentrate instead on civilian flying. He was now also acting as a father to four children, two siblings having been born after he and Pullman's mother had married. The part of North Wales they chose to live in was to provide Pullman with what he now remembers as 'a wonderful time':

> We lived up in the woods, about a mile above [a] very small village, right at the edge of a hill. We just wandered all over the place, there were no boundaries ... It was a time when children were allowed to and indeed expected, really, to leave the house after breakfast and not come back till darkness fell. And many times we did that. So I had a sort of wild and very unsupervised time, which was just great.

At school, while his brother was making model aeroplanes and volunteering for the Air Training Corps, Pullman preferred to spend his spare time reading, writing poetry, painting or strumming on his guitar. But from the age of thirteen he also came under the influence of Enid Jones, an inspired English teacher, to whom he still sends copies of his latest books. Her support and enthusiasm were important factors in helping him win a scholarship in 1965, after taking the entrance exams for Exeter College, Oxford, in order to study English. He was the first pupil from his school ever to go to Oxford University; winning a much-sought-after scholarship was an even more impressive achievement.

Although he had hoped that his time at university would further help him become an author, Pullman never found the inspiration there that he was looking for. Having fallen in love with the place on first visiting it while still at school, he felt badly let down by what he experienced as poor-quality teaching. He found lectures boring and there was an absence of any seminars where he could learn from, and debate with, other students. This meant that his only teaching contact each week was one hour with a tutor who never seemed interested in the first place. Pullman also grew increasingly restless with a system that demanded so much reading from one week to another while also providing so little time for adequate discussion.

After a year he applied to join a quite different course specialising in politics, philosophy and psychology. But his request was refused, and his final, disappointing, third-class degree was an indication of what can go wrong when a clever pupil is denied the sort of learning experience within which he or she can truly flourish. Pullman's often passionate engagement with educational issues since could well date back to this time. Excellent teaching at school then replaced by a university system where little tuition of real value ever seemed to happen was enough to make anyone angry.

There were plenty of good times though, with some acting in drama groups and folk-singing to his own guitar accompaniment. There was also 'a group of idle friends who occupied their time and mine betting on horses, getting drunk, and sprawling about telling creepy tales'. This life had something in common with Lyra's own time at Oxford, including her habit of crawling about on her college's roof:

> In my second year I occupied the rooms at the top of staircase 8, next to the lodge tower, and a friend, Jim Taylor, discovered that you could get out of the window and crawl along a very useful gutter behind the parapet. From there you could climb in through another window further along. I gave Lyra a better head for heights than I have, but I did the gutter crawl a number of times, usually when there was a party on the next staircase.

During his last year at university, Pullman came across the plot description on the back of Mikhail Bulgakov's famous pre-war Russian novel *The Master and Margarita*. This read: 'One hot spring the devil arrives in Moscow accompanied by a retinue that includes a beautiful naked witch and an immense talking black cat with a fondness for chess and vodka.' Without wanting to read the actual book, in case it interfered with the

4. Philip in top hat in *Doctor in the House*, aged sixteen. (Reproduced by kind permission of Philip Pullman.)

5. Exeter College, Oxford, on which the Jordan College of
His Dark Materials is based. The doorway to staircase 8 is on
the right of the main archway (in the centre of the photo).

workings of his own imagination, Pullman knew straightaway
that this mixture of the ordinary and the fantastic was what
he was looking for in his own writing, and decided there and
then to become a novelist. Starting to write his first book on
a beautiful summer morning the day after he left university,
Pullman got to page 70 of a magical-realistic story before he
was summoned to Uganda to look after his sick mother. He
told himself that if he could still get to page 100, he would
know that one day he would really become a proper author.
Writing his three pages a day, a habit he has maintained ever

since, he finally made his hundred pages before abandoning the story which he had now lost interest in, without even bothering to type it out.

With the vague idea of also becoming a singer-songwriter in his spare time, Pullman first worked in London at the gents's outfitters Moss Bros before trying his hand as an assistant librarian. A second novel followed, which won Pullman joint first prize in a literary competition designed for would-be writers below the age of 25. Described by Pullman as a metaphysical thriller, he now condemns this book as rubbish and wants nothing more to do with it. Finally training as a teacher, he married Judith Speller in 1970. For the next twelve years he taught children between 9 and 13, both at the rough end of Oxford and also in a more middle-class area.

One of his jobs was to put on the school play, and soon he was writing the material himself, ranging from comic melodrama to ghost stories. These productions were popular with parents as well as with pupils, giving Pullman his first hint that adults and children often enjoy the same sort of story so long as it is put over to them effectively. Turning the plays into published stories was a further step in his career as an author. At his second school, Pullman also had the job of stocking the school library. Initially he was doubtful whether parents would be willing to embrace some of the new realism in teenage fiction that was at this time causing some controversy. Summoning six parents from all walks of life to a meeting, Pullman handed out some of the more outspoken

6. Philip in beret, aged 25.
(Reproduced by kind permission of Philip Pullman.)

titles he particularly respected. He then asked them to read each title carefully, before deciding whether these were the sort of books they wanted for their children.

The results were extremely positive. Although occasionally shaken by the sometimes controversial choice of subject matter in this new writing, the parents all agreed at a further meeting that the authors in question were treating it sensitively and responsibly. There would therefore be no objections to such books appearing in the library. For Pullman, this was an extra significant victory. It signalled to him that writing for the young was now free from many of the restrictions that once used to bear down on authors trying to tell teenagers the truth as they saw it. This realisation was another important step in his decision to become a children's novelist himself.

Still writing three pages a day, Pullman's first illustrated children's novel, *Count Karlstein, or the Ride of the Demon Huntsman*, was published in 1972. He has since written that putting on this story first as a school play while he was still a teacher was the greatest fun he had ever had in his life. Ghosts, slapstick and special effects abounded in a story involving orphan fugitives, a wicked uncle and numerous near escapes. Narrated to her brother by Hildi, a brave and resourceful child, in some ways anticipating Lyra in the years to come, good finally overcomes evil in the most satisfying way. It was followed by a couple of adult novels, but Pullman only really hit his stride as a popular children's writer with *The Ruby in the Smoke*, published in 1985. Always a fan of Arthur

7. Philip, arms akimbo with walking stick, aged 26.
(Reproduced by kind permission of Philip Pullman.)

Conan Doyle's great detective Sherlock Holmes, he set out to write a similarly exciting crime story of the type that the children he had been teaching would really enjoy.

The end result was four gripping novels largely set in late 19th-century London, combining the traditional Victorian detective story with modern touches drawn from a range of popular films and fiction. Plots race along, packed with scenes

8. Patrice Aggs's final spread from the illustrated version of *Count Karlstein* (Philip Pullman, *Count Karlstein, or the Ride of the Demon Huntsman*, Corgi Yearling, 1991. Illustrations copyright © 1991 Patrice Aggs. Reproduced by permission of A.P. Watt Ltd on behalf of Patrice Aggs.)

of high drama and suspense. But Pullman also provides his own radical take on the social and political assumptions of that period. Evil is still represented by outsize villains, but also by social injustice and extreme poverty. Sally Lockhart, the lead character, starts as a sixteen-year-old orphan with a flair for detective work. Later an unmarried mother, after the murder of the man she loves, she is supported by a household of fellow workers. Like herself, these friends also operate mostly outside the norms of respectable society as it existed at the time.

Well received without ever becoming best-sellers, the first of the four titles were televised by the BBC in 2006, with Billie Piper playing Sally. A second instalment appeared a year later but there are no plans currently for televising the other two.

These and subsequent stories made it possible financially for Pullman to change to a part-time job at Westminster College, Oxford, where he was Senior Lecturer in English for the next eight years, retiring in 1996. This post involved teaching prospective teachers, with Pullman specialising in a course on storytelling. Training young teachers how to put across stories to children in the most effective way, Pullman used to narrate favourite tales himself by way of an object lesson, concentrating particularly on Greek myths. The fearsome harpies of Homer's *Odyssey* are not the only figures from these great myths to make a later appearance in *His Dark Materials*. The constant re-visiting of these most famous of stories also further convinced him of the appeal

9. Four illustrations from Victorian penny dreadfuls.
The melodrama of the penny dreadful is well captured

by Pullman's *Sally Lockhart* novels. (Reproduced
by permission of the British Library.)

good narrative has for all ages, given a clear plot and a lively sense of adventure – exactly the characteristics he was to take into his own writing.

Now with two sons, James and Thomas, he would henceforth spend each writing day shutting himself away in his shed at the bottom of the garden which – like Roald Dahl before him – gave him the temporary, total isolation he needed. He once said that if he were to have a dæmon – the type of animal guardian angel found throughout *His Dark Materials* – it would probably be a jackdaw or a magpie. His description of the particular shed in which he writes gives some idea as to why these particular birds came to mind:

My shed is a twelve foot by eight foot wooden structure, with electricity, insulation, heating, a carpet, the table where I write (which is covered in an old kilim rug), my exorbitantly expensive Danish tilting-in-all-directions orthopaedic gas-powered swivelling chair, my old computer, printer and scanner (i.e. they don't work anymore but I'm too mean to throw them out), manuscripts, drawings, apple cores, spiders' webs, dust, books in tottering heaps all over the floor and on every horizontal surface, about a thousand jiffy bags from books for review which I'm also too mean to throw away, a six-foot-long stuffed rat (the Giant Rat of Sumatra from a production of a Sherlock Holmes play I wrote for the Polka Theatre), a saxophone, a guitar, dozens of masks

10. Philip with his son Jamie, in about 1980.
(Reproduced by kind permission of Philip Pullman.)

PHILIP PULLMAN

of one sort or another, piles and piles of books and more books and still more books, a heater, an old armchair filled to capacity with yet more books, a filing cabinet that I haven't managed to open for eighteen months because of all the jiffy bags and books which have fallen in front of it in a sort of landslide, more manuscripts, more drawings, broken pencils, sharpened pencils, dust, dirt, bits of chewed carpet from when my young pug Hogarth comes to visit, stones of every kind: a cobblestone from Prague, a bit of Mont Blanc, a bit of Cape Cod ... On and on the list goes. It is a filthy abominable tip. No-one would go in there unless they absolutely had to. I enter it each morning with reluctance and leave as soon as I can.

This quotation provides a vivid impression of Pullman himself. Interested in everything that comes his way, self-deprecating but also very much his own master, quizzical, forthright and bursting with ideas, he is an excellent speaker as well as a brilliant writer. His enthusiasm even for the contents of his old shed is typical of his generally positive attitude towards the whole of life itself. He is also a generous man, always happy to praise those other children's authors that he reads and enjoys. When he writes in *His Dark Materials* that heaven should be seen not as another place but as very much where we are at the moment, there is no doubt that he is also referring to the continual joy he

28

finds in his own life, not least in his own family and in the later arrival of four grandchildren.

The Firework-Maker's Daughter, published in 1995, once again has a sparky girl as its heroine. Unable to become a recognised firework-maker because of her sex, she still triumphs through courage and determination, seeing off an initially terrifying visit to the great Razvani, residing in his so-called Grotto of the Fire-Fiend. Once there she encounters a procession of weeping and wailing ghosts, anticipating the haunted spirits later found in *His Dark Materials*. She also discovers that the flames apparently surrounding Razvani are illusions, as he is the first to agree. Winner of the Smarties Book Prize for that year, it was adapted for the operatic stage in 2013 by composers Glyn Maxwell and David Bruce, receiving its first performances at The Royal Opera House.

Just as successful, *Clockwork, or All Wound Up*, published the following year, is another splendidly spooky tale aimed at young readers. It features a murderous wind-up model and a young prince with a mechanical heart that is gradually rusting away. The villain is Karl, a sullen apprentice who enters into a pact with the devil. He is eventually murdered by his own ingeniously created robot. Gretl, an innkeeper's daughter, also plays a leading role. Pullman also showed evidence here of becoming interested in some of the broader issues raised in this otherwise cheerfully melodramatic story.

The whole idea of a wind-up robot that has no choice but to obey is linked by him to Isaac Newton's model of a mechanistic universe, within which one scientific event will always necessarily follow another when the same conditions apply. But since the development of the study of quantum mechanics, scientists now take a much less deterministic view of why things happen as they do. Pullman has always been up to date with these intellectual changes, attracted to the idea that the inherent instability of all matter ensures there will always be uncertainty when it comes to understanding the world we live in. He therefore makes light of mechanistic theories in one of the boxes for the author's own comments scattered throughout the text of this story. But towards the end he also suggests that in storytelling the reverse is true. Once a narrator has created characters, they must then follow particular paths because of the people they are. In this sense, Pullman is declaring himself as an author still writing in the tradition where characters largely do as they are told by a narrator holding all the cards. Moments of ambiguity and textual uncertainty are not and never have been for him. The same could be said of his moral outlook in his fiction, where good and bad characters are clearly announced from the start and tend to stay that way for the rest of the story.

Throughout the story, other opinions of Pullman's are also included in different boxes, on topics ranging from clock-work figures in general, to the artistic temperament, the soul, winning and losing, doctors, wolves and anything else that takes his fancy. These boxes are reminiscent of those odd facts or digressions that teachers sometimes slip into their

ADVERTISEMENT

"ANTI BUGGO"

THE INSECTS' DESPAIR...

In Aggs's Patent steam-powered Combination Insecticide Diffuser and Musical Companion.

ZAMIEL SHOE REPAIRS

NEW SOLES FOR OLD

Devilish good service

Feeling the chill? Wear

"ST ELMO"

Electric undergarments. Shockingly effective!

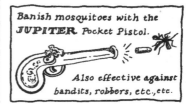

Banish mosquitoes with the JUPITER Pocket Pistol.

Also effective against bandits, robbers, etc., etc.

Get your pet back on her hooves with

BEEFO
Animal Stimulant.

By the makers of Doggo, Catto, Horso, etc.

11. Patrice Aggs's advertisement appears at the back of the illustrated version of *Count Karlstein* (Philip Pullman, *Count Karlstein, or the Ride of the Demon Huntsman*, Corgi Yearling, 1991. Illustrations copyright © 1991 Patrice Aggs. Reproduced by permission of A.P. Watt Ltd on behalf of Patrice Aggs.)

lessons to keep their pupils interested, suggesting what a very good teacher Pullman himself must have been. But they also indicate an author ready to move on to fiction dealing with more complex issues aimed at adult readers as well as at older children.

His next illustrated story for younger readers, *I was a Rat! Or The Scarlet Slippers* was the first of his books to be made into a full-length film by the BBC in 2001. Its main character is one of the rats that was changed into a pageboy in the story of *Cinderella* but who never manages to change back again. Kidnapped by an unscrupulous showman, he escapes to join a band of young robbers and after being caught is condemned to death. But he is saved by the Princess Aurelia, whose secret is that she is the former Cinderella. But she confesses to the rat boy, that being a princess is not all it is cracked up to be. 'I don't think it's what you *are* that matters,' she tells him. 'I think it's what you *do.*'

Elsewhere in the story attacks on pompous, unfeeling authority, insensitive teachers, vindictive newspapers and bleak orphanages are all typical of an author who is always on the side of the vulnerable and misunderstood. Hope resides with those humans for whom love and kindness are more important than greed and power. Although this story ends happily, there are also moments that have much in common with sections of *His Dark Materials*, particularly the image of an orphaned child up against a heartless organisation, which has overtones of Lyra's plight. The decision taken at one point to exterminate the rat boy recalls the similarly pitiless cruelty shown by the scientists and their masters in the hideous camp where Lyra is briefly imprisoned.

Pullman's life changed altogether with the publication of *Northern Lights* in 1995 (titled *The Golden Compass* in America), *The Subtle Knife* in 1997 and *The Amber Spyglass* in 2000. *His Dark Materials*, the name given to this great trilogy, went on to sell fifteen million copies and was translated into 40 languages, leaving him with a secure income and therefore the option to go on writing whenever and whatever he liked. This best-selling work was also a critical success. In 1996 *Northern Lights* won both the Carnegie Medal and the Guardian's Children's Fiction Prize. In 2001 *The Amber Spyglass* won the Whitbread Book of the Year Award (now known as the Costa Award), the first time this prize has ever been awarded for a children's book. In 2003 *His Dark Materials* was adapted in two parts for the stage by Nicholas Wright, opening at London's National Theatre to packed houses. Produced by Nicholas Hytner, Anna Maxwell Martin played Lyra, Patricia Hodge took on Mrs Coulter and Timothy Dalton was an appropriately smouldering Lord Asriel. Dæmons were designed by Michael Curry, appearing as shapes lit from within worked by silent operators dressed in black.

In the same year the BBC presented the trilogy on Radio 4, adapted into three radio plays. It also issued a complete recording of the trilogy on audiobook, narrated by the author and with a cast including Joanna Wyatt as Lyra, Alison Dowling as Mrs Coulter and Sean Barrett reading both Lord Asriel and Iorek the bear. In 2004 Pullman was granted a CBE in the New Year's Honours list, and a number of universities have awarded him honorary degrees since. In 2007, *The Golden Compass*, a film adaptation of *Northern Lights*, was released. Admired for its special effects, it was not an outstanding critical or box office success, and future plans for filming the other two novels of the trilogy were finally abandoned.

In 2006 *Northern Lights* was chosen by readers as the Carnegie of Carnegies, out of all the other titles that have won this coveted medal since it was first awarded in 1936. More writing also followed, and in 2007 Pullman started on *The Book of Dust*, a three volume work relating to *His Dark Materials*, with the first instalment appearing in 2017. To those who have previously accused him of only focusing on the evils of organised religion he has said: 'This is a big subject and I'm writing a big, big book in order to deal precisely with that question.'

Ill health since 2007 has been a factor in this long writing process, along with time off that he could now afford to take in order to continue with other interests, such as wood carving and illustration, with these skills on view in the tiny pictures opposite chapter headings in *Northern Lights* and *The Subtle Knife*. He has also greatly enjoyed writing the text for a comic strip story, *The Adventures of John Blake:*

Mystery of the Ghost Ship. Illustrated by Fred Fordham and serialised in *The Phoenix*, an up-market weekly British comic, the whole story first appeared in Britain and America as a graphic novel in early 2017. Once again, different times and places become an issue as John Blake, a research scientist, is condemned to sail between the centuries after an experiment goes badly wrong. Up against him is the all-powerful Dahlberg Corporation, whose evil intentions constitute a terrible threat to all concerned.

Pullman has also taken up a number of causes during the last two decades. Elected President of the Society of Authors, he has written eloquently against what he saw as the crippling restrictiveness running through the recommendations of the National Curriculum where the teaching of English was concerned. Nearer home, he joined protests about the proposal to build new accommodation on the site of Castle Mill, the last working boatyard on the Oxford canal. He described this as 'a watery, raffish, amiable, trickster-like world of boat dwellers and horse dealers and alchemists – very ancient, quite unmistakable, entirely unique.' Much of Lyra's early adventures in *Northern Lights* took place in identical surroundings. The proposal still went through, though with some modifications.

He has also been a vocal campaigner on a number of other issues. In 2008, he led a campaign against the introduction of age bands on the covers of children's books, saying: 'It's based on a one-dimensional view of growth, which regards growing older as moving along a line like a monkey climbing a stick:

now you're seven, so you read these books; and now you're nine so you read these.' More than 1,200 authors, booksellers, illustrators, librarians and teachers joined this campaign.

In 2014, he supported the Let Books Be Books campaign to stop children's books being labelled as 'for girls' or 'for boys', saying: 'I'm against anything, from age-ranging to pinking and blueing, whose effect is to shut the door in the face of children who might enjoy coming in. No publisher should announce on the cover of any book the sort of readers the book would prefer. Let the readers decide for themselves.' He and other authors also threatened to stop visiting schools in protest at new laws requiring them to be vetted to work with youngsters. Before that, in 2011, he backed a campaign to stop 600 library closures in England calling it a 'war against stupidity.' Speaking at a conference organised by The Library Campaign, he insisted that:

'The book is second only to the wheel as the best piece of technology human beings have ever invented. A book symbolises the whole intellectual history of mankind; it's the greatest weapon ever devised in the war against stupidity. Beware of anyone who tries to make books harder to get at. And that is exactly what these closures are going to do – oh, not intentionally, except in a few cases; very few people are stupid intentionally; but that will be the effect. Books will be harder to get at. Stupidity will gain a little ground.'

As a long-time enthusiast of William Blake, and president of the Blake Society, Pullman led a campaign in 2014 to buy the Sussex cottage in Felpham where the poet lived for three years. For Pullman: 'It isn't beyond the resources of a nation that can spend enormous amounts of money on acts of folly and unnecessary warfare, a nation that likes to boast about its literary heritage, to find the money to pay for a proper memorial and a centre for the study of this great poet and artist.' In 2015 the little house, where Blake originally wrote 'And did those feet in ancient time' was finally bought for public use by the Blake Society.

Pullman is an emotional man, laughing, shuddering and on occasions weeping over his stories as they unfold. His main characters often seem to make their presence known to him almost personally. In the case of Lyra in *His Dark Materials*, he has said it was as if he could hear her voice and knew precisely what she looked like. Left wing in his politics, he sees his writing as part of a dissenting tradition stretching back once again to his particular hero William Blake.

A central part of Pullman's philosophy as a writer is that people should be judged by what they do rather than what they say. This rests upon another assumption, which is that since everyone always has the power of choice, it is up to them to see that they make the right ones. His own life could be seen as an example of someone who has chosen the positive rather than the negative path. An unsettled childhood involving constant moves, a succession of new schools, a dead father, a stepfather and an often absent mother could have been seen as reason for resentment, both at the time and later on as well.

But Pullman has no such reservations, always choosing to celebrate the positive features of his life to date. For some, such optimism smacks of denial, with Pullman unwilling to register the anger and depression he might once have felt as a child, preferring instead to express it in his writing when it comes to portraying generally hateful villains. For others, probably including Pullman himself, his life is a story within which the love of important others plus the powers of his own imagination have provided all that he needed, both as man and boy. Taking the position that individuals – including himself – always have the power and ability to be ultimately responsible for the course of their own lives has enabled Pullman to write the positive stories that he has. This type of inner conviction, linked to his extraordinary powers of imagination, has been welcomed by multitudes of readers, both young and old. There have always been others, both in life and in literature, who take a far bleaker view of the power of any individual to shape their own lives to any significant degree. Pullman has never been one of these and has little sympathy with those who take this pessimistic view, particularly if they should also be writing for younger audiences in need of hope and belief at this stage of their lives.

But Pullman cannot be written off as the type of born optimist who can always find a positive in everything. He has also had experience of depression, which he has described as a time when 'life and the meaning and the colour drains out of everything and leaves you indifferent, indifferent to your own self as well as anyone else'. He says more about this in a dialogue with Marie Bridge, as part of a series of conversations with authors and psychoanalysts held at the Institute of Psychoanalysis in 2003. He admits that his description of the feelings suffered by the witch Lena Feldt in *The Subtle Knife* after her dæmon was ravaged by a Spectre also represents his own personal experience of bad times too:

> She felt a nausea of the soul, a hideous and sickening despair, a melancholy weariness so profound that she was going to die of it. Her last conscious thought was disgust with life: her senses had lied to her. The world was not made of energy and delight but of foulness, betrayal, and lassitude. Living was hateful and death was no better, and from end to end of the universe, this was the first and last and only truth.

Yet he still insists that the personal journey from initial innocence to ultimate wisdom always remains possible despite such hazards along the way. Following the German philosopher-writer Heinrich von Kleist, about whom more later, Pullman explains to his audience of psychoanalysts that the only way to re-enter the lost Paradise of childhood innocence is to 'Go all the way around the world experiencing life and suffering and sorrow and trouble and difficulty, but learning all the while until eventually, if you live long enough, you will re-enter Paradise, as it were through the back door.' And for Pullman in particular, the greatest stories offer the best guides as to what we can strive to achieve as humans over the course of a lifetime.

The particular journeys his main characters have to take in order to arrive where they want to be are indeed often of necessity hard and testing, requiring constant courage as well as an unwavering – though not unquestioning – faith in the whole enterprise at all stages. The temptation to give up at any time can only be countered by making a renewed effort, even in the toughest of conditions. If and when a particular battle is finally won, it may be at some personal cost. So although Pullman chooses a fantasy setting for his most important novels, his main characters still basically achieve their ends through hard work. The same could also be said of the author himself, shut away in his shed at the bottom of the garden and not allowing himself to leave until he has written the three pages per day that finally meet with the stringent and ever-demanding standards of his artistic approval.

12. Philip Pullman, taken c.1997.
(Reproduced by permission of Scholastic Ltd.)

His Dark Materials

The Stories

Pullman's great trilogy was written over a period of seven years and is around 1,300 pages long. Its cast ranges from scholarly Oxford dons to armoured bears, witches, angels, murderous Spectres and hideous harpies. It can be read at many different levels, from an adventure story to a parable about the essence of human nature and how this has been betrayed. As he puts it himself, it is also a story about what it means 'to be human, to grow up, to suffer, and to learn'. It draws on a wide range of sources, from Ancient Greek myths, the Bible, Dante, John Milton and William Blake to Hollywood films, a Finnish telephone directory and the superstring theory developed from the study of quantum physics.

Partly arising from a suggestion by Pullman over lunch with his editor David Fickling that his next project might involve a re-writing of Milton's *Paradise Lost*, the trilogy also draws on and develops themes and ideas found in his previous

novels. Although it brings numbers of philosophical and scientific ideas into play, it is at base a work of imagination and
should always be read as such. For Pullman, the story comes
first before everything else, and he strongly believes that it
is through stories that humans can best hope to understand
both themselves and others. As a writer who has never gone
in for too much forward planning, he also believes that as the
story itself emerges, it always knows best, even when it may
occasionally seem to be going in an unexpected direction.
Sometimes the extra meaning implicit in what he has written, in terms of how it then goes on to inform what happens
in the rest of the trilogy, has only become clear to him well
after the event.

The basic plot of the trilogy describes how two children,
Lyra and Will, manage to overcome forces of oppression
to establish a new order based on truth, honesty and love.
In so doing, they repeat the original decision of Adam and
Eve to seek full understanding and consciousness by eating
from the tree of knowledge. But this time the two children, in
their own symbolic re-enactment of this original act of defi-
ance, manage to defeat a Church establishment which is still
intent on condemning their determined search for freedom
as a wicked rebellion. Involving a whole universe of different
human, animal and supernatural players inhabiting a number
of parallel worlds, Will and Lyra also have to sort out some
personal difficulties with their own parents. They must, too,
make a final decision about their growing feelings for each

13. 'Nearer he drew, and many a walk traversed /
Of stateliest covert, cedar, pine or palm.' (IX 434–435)
(Source: *Doré's Illustrations for 'Paradise Lost'*, Gustave
Doré. Copyright © 1993 by Dover Publications, Inc.)

other, when it becomes clear that it will not be possible for them to live together in the same world now made fresh and new by their joint victory.

Northern Lights

This story opens with eleven-year-old Lyra Belacqua, accompanied as always by her dæmon Pantalaimon. This is the inseparable, visible spirit that is part of every child in her particular world and can change into any sort of animal. Only later, when an individual turns adult, does the dæmon finally stay in a fixed form for the rest of their life. Lyra and her dæmon are creeping through the darkened main hall of Jordan College, Oxford.

As there is no such college, this is in a world which, as the author says, is 'like ours, but different in many ways'. Overhearing a plot by the Master of the College to poison Lord Asriel, the man she believes to be her uncle but who is in fact her father, Lyra prevents him from drinking a fatal draught. After that, she hears Lord Asriel tell colleagues about his discovery of another world running parallel with this one and his determination to explore it. He also talks about Dust, the normally invisible particles that cluster around living beings. During the rest of the evening, the Master of the College is forced to give up his plans to stop Lord Asriel's supposedly dangerous enquiries from going any further.

In the coming weeks, Lyra becomes aware that some local children have been mysteriously disappearing, including her particular friend Roger, a kitchen boy and the son of a college servant. She also makes the acquaintance of the glamorous Mrs Coulter, without knowing that Mrs Coulter is her mother. Mrs Coulter then plans to take Lyra with her on an exciting journey to the North. But before this happens, the Master of the College, in conditions of the greatest secrecy, presents Lyra with an alethiometer, which he hopes will help protect her from the terrible dangers Lord Asriel seems intent on drawing both himself and his daughter into. Once she has learned to read it, this device will provide her with honest and accurate answers to all the questions she puts to it.

Things soon turn sour with Mrs Coulter, when Lyra learns that she plays an important role in the Church's General Oblation Board. This organisation has been supervising the kidnapping of children from Oxford and elsewhere. The children are then taken far North to Bolvangar, where Lord Asriel is being held captive as well. Lyra runs away to try to free him. She makes contact with John Faa, the leader of the Oxford Gyptians, some tough water gypsies with whom Lyra has had numbers of high-spirited disputes in the past. But everyone is united now in the determination to find the missing children, and Lyra joins an expedition setting out to rescue them. While she is with the Gyptians, she finally learns the truth about who her parents are after talking to John Faa and his aged companion, Farder Coram.

Once the group reaches Lapland, Lyra meets Iorek Byrnison, a talking, armoured bear. He tells them where the lost children are being kept, and how they are being cut away from their dæmons in a hideous operation known as intercision. The Gyptians also meet the American aviator

Lee Scoresby. He is named by Pullman after the actor Lee Van Cleef, who appeared in a number of films with Clint Eastwood, and William Scoresby, a real-life Arctic explorer. They hire him and his balloon for extra back-up. Lyra becomes friends with Serafina Pekkala too, a witch queen who reveals Lyra's own particular destiny, which is to bring an end to destiny itself. The witch's surname was drawn by Pullman at random from a Finnish phone directory.

As they near their destination, Lyra is kidnapped by a band of Tartars who take her to the special camp which houses the lost children. Scientists hired by the Church Oblation Board are removing the dæmons from the children who have been rounded up before they can reach adolescence. The Church believes that dæmons help attract Dust to the individual concerned, and that this Dust is synonymous with original sin. But Pullman describes Dust instead as the essence of all accumulated human consciousness. It is attracted to adults rather than to children since older people are less innocent and more experienced. If a dæmon is cut away before a child enters puberty, then Dust would no longer be drawn towards the same child once turned adult. And without dæmons everyone becomes much tamer and more manageable, so providing the Church with no trouble when it comes to maintaining and extending what in this world still remained its traditional near-total control.

Hiding under an assumed name after she hears that her mother has arrived at the camp, Lyra meets up again with

Roger. Mrs Coulter then rescues her daughter when Lyra is about to be forced to undergo the operation herself. But her mother also wants to get her hands on Lyra's alethiometer. With the help of Iorek the bear plus an army of friendly witches headed by Serafina Pekkala, Lyra escapes with Roger in Lee Scoresby's balloon. This is then attacked by hordes of cliff-ghasts: large, venomous creatures with leather wings and hooked claws. Crashing to earth, Lyra is captured by another tribe of bears who turn out to be hostile. Tricking them into allowing Iorek into their midst, Lyra sees her great friend beat his rival Iofur in single combat. He can now once again take up his rightful leadership of this particular kingdom of the bears.

Lyra then finds Lord Asriel in order to give him the alethiometer she thought he needed, though he can now do without it. In return, he tells her of the great battle that led to the Church condemning Dust as a manifestation of the original sin committed when Eve ate the apple from the tree of knowledge in the Garden of Eden. He now wants to travel to other worlds in order to trace the origin of all Dust. But when Lyra wakes up after a night's rest, she finds that her father has departed, taking Roger with him. For in order to travel to another world, her father needs that flash of extra energy generated when a child is separated from his or her dæmon. Roger has been chosen to pay this heavy price. Too late to intervene, Lyra follows him and her father into another world, determined now to find out for herself what Dust is all about.

With an attempted murder in the first chapter, along with rumours of an imminent global war, *Northern Lights* gets off to a running start and maintains a fierce narrative pace to the end. Familiar conventions of children's adventure stories abound, such as vital eavesdropping, kidnapping, rescues, last-minute escapes and hiding away to avoid capture. There are also some graphic fights involving victory over villainous-looking adversaries. Events on the emotional front are equally gripping, with a wicked mother pretending to be nice and a sulky father intent on getting his own way whatever the outcome. The main character, Lyra, who has to cope with all these situations is an immediately attractive presence, mischievous but brave, and at home within a wide social spectrum. Shrugging off any adult who tries to control her, she relishes the sort of independence denied to most children, who have always enjoyed reading about wild adventures within the consoling safety of their own homes.

If this were all, Pullman would have written a serviceable but unexceptional adventure story using well-grounded but familiar plot devices. But by introducing the concept of Dust early on he brings in a new and highly charged dimension, full of meaning but ambiguous at the same time. Lyra is understandably puzzled by this phenomenon but is determined to find out more about it. More ominously for her, it seems as if she has also been chosen by the fates, whatever they are, to bring about the end of destiny itself. The universe, as cranky Professor Jotham Santelia explains to her towards the end, 'is full of *intentions*.' Never quite sure what these intentions might be, Lyra and her readers advance towards the second volume knowing there is still all to play for.

The Subtle Knife

The narrative starts with Will Parry, a twelve-year-old boy living in modern-day England. Following the disappearance of his explorer-father John on an expedition to the North, Will now has to look after his mentally ill mother. He is taking her to a place of safety after their house has been raided by two sinister men intent on stealing a case of letters and documents belonging to his father. Will foils them, but rightly fears he may have unintentionally killed one of the men.

Running away after leaving his mother in the care of a kind, older friend, he comes across an almost invisible window in the air while walking through the Northern suburbs of Oxford. Passing through it, he finds he is in Cittàgazze, literally the city of the magpies, which acts as a type of crossroads between millions of different worlds. It is an eerie, empty, Italian type of town, only inhabited by children because of the existence of ghost-like Spectres that have fed on all the adults there, leaving them as zombies. There he meets Lyra, also lost in this alien world.

Returning together to Will's Oxford, Lyra meets Dr Mary Malone, a scientist working in the university's Dark Matter Research Unit. Dark matter here is defined as the so-far undetected stuff that exists between stars and makes gravity work, and which makes up at least 90 per cent of the universe. Lyra tells her about Dust, and together the two are able to bring up on a computer screen some elementary particles that seem to have consciousness. Dark matter and Dust turn out to be one and the same thing, or as the angel Balthamos puts it later: 'Dust is only a name for what happens when matter begins to understand itself.'

Lyra loses her alethiometer to Lord Boreal, a smooth-tongued, dishonest collector. He will only give it back if she and Will bring him the very special knife that exists in the other, Italian, world. Returning to Cittàgazze, they finally capture the knife during a fight in the Torre degli Angeli, the Tower of the Angels, formerly occupied by the local Guild of Philosophers.

Will is wounded in the process, losing two fingers and then bleeding dangerously. Like many other traditional heroes, he has to pay a harsh price in acquiring the magical powers he needs. He soon manages to learn how to operate the knife, which is capable of cutting a window into another world at a moment's notice. By now Will has read the letters his father sent home during his final expedition, where he too wrote about the windows that exist between worlds. Will decides that his father may still be alive, and resolves to find him. Back in Oxford, the two children use the knife to cut their way from one world to another, so allowing them access to Lord Boreal's house, where they steal back the alethiometer. Lord Boreal is entertaining Mrs Coulter at the time, who is still anxious to find Lyra.

Meanwhile Lee Scoresby, the aviator, has met up with Stanislaus Grumman, who turns out to be John Parry, Will's father and now a self-taught shaman. Grumman too has been investigating Dust, which was why the two hired men, acting on instructions from the Church, were trying to confiscate his papers at the start of the story. He also knows about the knife, though not that it is his own son who currently holds it. Grumman desperately wants to find whoever does have it, in order to tell him or her about the vital role it has to play in the future fate of the entire universe.

The soldiers of the Church surround Lee and shoot him dead after a prolonged gun battle. Will at last meets his father, who tells him that the knife is the only weapon capable of killing God himself. But just as they finally both recognise each other, John Parry is slain by the witch he once dared to scorn. Will is then told by two angels to find Lord Asriel, in order to help him in his great fight against the Church authorities. But Lyra meanwhile has disappeared, and Will wonders if he is ever going to see her again.

Evil in its blackest form again walks the land here, with ghastly Spectres not unlike the Dementors that haunt J.K. Rowling's *Harry Potter* stories. In each case, they have the power to invade and destroy a person, rendering them into a zombie state. Evil is shown to exist in children too, with Lyra declaring to Will that she will never trust kids again, after seeing the young people of Cittàgazze torturing and killing a pet cat. In return, Will tells her about the time when his mentally ill mother was tormented by boys from his school.

For Will, this could be evidence that: 'Maybe we do have the Spectres in my world, only we can't see them and we haven't got a name for them.' Other explanations for the existence of evil in humans go back as far as the Bible and beyond. Pullman rejects theological theories as to why this should be, and is happy to describe various communities, such as the Gyptians, where harmony always prevails. He is also a life-long admirer of Erich Kästner's pre-war classic children's tale *Emil and the Detectives*, where a group of street-wise Berlin children set about helping the more innocent country-born Emil track down the crook who has stolen his money. For Pullman, the main point in this junior self-help story is 'that the children find the solution themselves, out of the everyday qualities they share: resourcefulness, quick wits, determination.' The same could equally be said about the Oxford urchins with whom Lyra has such close connections in the previous volume. Although mischievous, they always work together when the occasion demands.

But this still leaves us with other characters, junior and senior, capable of appalling behaviour without conscience or regret. It would be unfair to expect Pullman to come up with any easy theory about why humans in both life and his stories are at times given to general wickedness. The existence of such characters certainly makes for stirring moments when they can be roundly defeated by the good, to every reader's satisfaction. But despite Pullman's ingenious reworking of the Bible story to show how things could once have been much better, there is no indication in his stories that all evil can simply be blamed on the noxious influence of a perverted religion. Other forces are clearly involved too, but of these we hear little at any stage.

On another tack, there are also powerful warnings here about what a world could look like after extreme climate change, when the summers have become hotter than they used to be after adverse reaction to chemicals injected into the atmosphere. Altogether, things are looking very bleak at the conclusion of this story. Time to move on to the final instalment.

The Amber Spyglass

L yra is drugged and kept captive by her mother in a secret cave. Mrs Coulter had snatched her daughter away in order to save Lyra from the Church, which wants to kill the child whom it now views as a second Eve. Just as the first Eve was judged to have made trouble by disobeying God's orders, Lyra too is seen as a potential rebel who could, if left alone, re-write human history. Mrs Coulter wants to save her, even though this means opposing the Church for which she had worked so diligently in the past.

Will is still being urged to find Lord Asriel by the two angels, Balthamos and Baruch. They also had previously taken sides against the ultimate Authority, variously known as 'God, the Creator, the Lord, Yahweh, El, Adonai, the King, the Father, the Almighty'. As Balthamos points out: 'He was never the creator. He was an angel like ourselves – the first angel, true, the most powerful, but he was formed of Dust as we are, and Dust is only a name for what happens when matter begins to understand itself.'

It was this same grim Authority that banished the original Eve after she discovered that he was in fact not the Creator at all. This Authority was later backed by the established Church. His second in command, Metatron, is now out to kill both Will and Lyra. But Will is determined to find Lyra first, as are Iorek the bear, Serafina Pekkala the witch and Lord Roke, Lord Asriel's spy-captain. This gallant gentleman, no taller than six inches, rides on a dragonfly and is the possessor of a lethal pair of poisoned spurs. A new character, Father Gomez, is also in on the hunt. He has a special commission from the Church's Consistorial Court of Discipline to find and eliminate Lyra as soon as possible.

The action then passes to Mary Malone, alone in a world not her own. She meets the strange *mulefa*, peaceful talking animals with horned heads and short trunks who travel around with the aid of two wheel-shaped seed-pods. Their gentle placidity is reminiscent of the Moomin characters invented by the Finnish children's author Tove Jansson, much admired by Pullman as a self-evident genius. But the mulefa are now perpetually raided by cruel, giant bird-shaped creatures known as the *tualapi*. The trees upon which the mulefa depend for their seed-pods are also dying because their world is losing the vital Dust that once allowed it to thrive.

Will locates Lyra, but is nearly taken in by Mrs Coulter's charm. His attempt to rescue her daughter works, although his knife gets broken in the process. Lyra then dreams that Roger, her former friend, wants urgently to speak to her, which will necessitate a trip to the land of the dead. After Iorek mends Will's knife, Lyra and Will join a procession of ghosts making their way to the underworld. But when they get to the river dividing the living from the dead, Lyra discovers that she has to leave behind her beloved dæmon, such an integral part of herself. This is the great sacrifice originally mentioned by the Master of Jordan College, when he revealed that the alethiometer had prophesied that at some stage Lyra would perform an act of terrible betrayal. But she has to do so, agonising and unbearable though it is.

After the crossing she meets Roger, now like her without his dæmon. They encounter some terrifying half-human, half-animal harpies, appointed by the Authority to torment the ghosts of the dead with reminders of all their former wickedness, cruelty and greed. This ghastly process happens to everyone who dies, good or bad alike, because up to now the land of the dead is far from being anything like heaven. It is in fact a place of nothing, 'with no hope of freedom, or joy, or sleep or rest or peace'.

Lyra finds she can get round the harpies by telling them stories that are true at heart. Won over by their enjoyment of these tales, the harpies agree to conduct all future ghosts to the special exit from the underworld that Will and Lyra are planning to make. But this is only on condition that the ghosts involved continue to tell them stories about the lives they once had on earth, true stories about what they have 'seen and heard and loved and known in the world'. Once they leave the land of the dead, they can then happily disappear and in so doing become at one with all other living things on earth. As they approach this moment of final liberation, Will has one last encounter with his father, now also a ghost.

Mrs Coulter meanwhile has made her way to the President of the Consistorial Court of Discipline, who operates from Geneva. She is imprisoned, but discovers that the President is overseeing the making of a bomb that will kill Lyra once exploded, since it contains a lock of her hair which, with the advanced technology involved, is enough to enable it to track her down. Mrs Coulter just succeeds in aborting this bomb, and is then rescued, bruised and bleeding, by Lord Asriel. They resolve their differences, each determined to keep Lyra alive at all costs against the different threats facing her.

To this end, Mrs Coulter arranges to meet, and then pretends to seduce, Metatron, The Authority's Regent and the greatest of Lyra's enemies. She tells him she wants to betray her daughter, but this is a ruse to enable Lord Asriel to first ambush and then hurl the wicked angel into an abyss from which there is no return. But he can only do this by sacrificing his own life at the same time, as does Mrs Coulter, having finally admitted to herself that her love for Lyra is now greater than her own wish for survival.

Reunited with Mary Malone, Lyra and Will learn that Dust is leaking from this world because there are now so many windows leading off from it. Will therefore has the duty of closing them, except for one through which the ghosts of the dead can continually pass into the living world before finally disappearing. Father Gomez, Lyra's would-be assassin, is stopped and then killed at the last moment by the angel Balthamos. Lyra and Will find their dæmons once again, and Will is able to see his for the first time.

They realise that they are now in love, but because of the necessity for closing the windows that exist between their two worlds, it will not be possible for them to live together. The option of one staying in the other's world is impossible, since any prolonged absence from one's own universe inevitably leads to premature old age and death. Instead, Lyra will go to school for the first time in her Oxford, while Will must first destroy his knife and then return to the mother who needs him so much in his own world. But they will never forget the great love they have for each other, and both are now determined to help build the Republic of Heaven on earth, by which they understand that they are making the very best of the life they currently possess, both for themselves and for others.

In this story, Pullman gives his final clues about the greater meaning of his trilogy. Rejecting orthodox Christianity he also recognises the spiritual loneliness experienced by Mary Malone and others, of living in what they have come to believe is a Godless universe. His answer is an insistence instead on continuing to celebrate the best of what life and the world still have to offer. Simple, sensual pleasures are pictured as properly and significantly life-affirming. Or, as Lyra experiences it after waking up from a long sleep out of doors: 'She felt the little breeze and the sun's warmth and she heard the little insect-scrapings and the bell-song of that bird high above. It was all good. She had forgotten how good the world was.'

The onset of sexuality is for Pullman another moment of huge human potential. Sexual attraction and fulfilment, demonised in the traditional Adam and Eve story, is seen instead as the greatest adventure of them all. When Mary Malone recounts what she describes as the paradise of her own first adult sexual experience, Lyra, listening enrapt,

> felt as if she had been handed the key to a great house that was somehow inside her, and as she turned the key, deep in the darkness of the building she felt other doors opening too, and lights coming on … And inside her, that rich house with all its doors open and all its rooms lit stood waiting, quiet, expectant.

Lyra and Will are both under-age, and Pullman is writing principally for a junior audience. So their own sexual awakening is merely signalled by the symbolism of Lyra offering Will a little red fruit just as Eve once gave Adam the famous apple. But this time the couple are allowed to celebrate their burgeoning love for each other without guilt. Later on, in another symbolic act, they shyly handle each other's dæmons. Their final parting is even more painful, but Pullman insists that they can still go on to live good lives apart.

For Mary Malone, also at the end of her story: 'The clouds seemed to *know* what they were doing and why, and the wind knew, and the grass knew. The entire world was alive and conscious.' But while she felt the truth of this observation, she herself still did not know what this ultimate purpose was. Pullman too, also coming to the end of his own particular fictional journey, is in something of the same position.

Outspoken about what he sees as poisonous ways of viewing the human's place in the universe, he feels instead that there is a positive message out there for us all but one that can only be experienced at best instinctively by leading good, positive lives.

To get this view across, he uses his own God-like role as narrator to advance the causes of those he sees as the good and condemn those he has written off as the bad. The prophecies surrounding Lyra and Will and their ultimate destiny come true not through any revealed intervention from a higher force, but because Pullman wills them so. He also uses details and characters from great stories from the past, including some from what Mary Malone later describes as 'that very powerful and convincing mistake, Christianity'.

So here is a humanist writer who still reaches for the Bible, even if it means re-writing crucial scenes. Pullman has always seen himself as, above everything else, a storyteller. And if the story fits his writer's purpose he will include it, whatever its genesis. There is, after all, a wisdom in the greatest stories that have survived over the centuries. They can give meaning where there is confusion and hope where there is despair. Above all, they help define what it is to be human by our reactions to them. Lyra, like her author, is also a born storyteller. The stories she tells and the visions she has ultimately work for everyone's good. His many fans might well claim that the same could be said of Pullman himself.

Will and Lyra

L yra is a character immediately recognisable from some of Pullman's earlier stories. Mischievous, tough-minded, disrespectful and independent, she is also kind and caring when it most matters. Moving easily between the social classes, she is at home with everyone willing to treat her as a proper person in her own right. No respecter of adult authority, enjoying anarchic mud fights and often in need of a good wash and brush-up, there are moments when, like the character Thunderbolt in the *New Cut Gang* stories, she reminds readers of Richmal Crompton's pre-war child character William.

Spitting plum stones onto the heads of passing scholars or hooting like an owl outside a window where a tutorial is going on are both activities enjoyed by Lyra that William would have been proud to imitate. Cousins, the Master of Jordan's manservant, is at one moment described as 'an old enemy of Lyra's'. This phrase is identical to the descriptions of

William's various adult adversaries. Lyra's child friends, and the often ungrammatical English with which they speak to each other, also have something in common with the mode of speech used by William's band of self-styled Outlaws: a gang of children as mischievous as he is himself.

Although Lyra is no orphan, she has had an orphan's upbringing, having been falsely told that her parents had died in an airship accident. Her childhood has been supervised by those living or working in the all-male Jordan College. There is also help from Mrs Lonsdale, a hard-working but unaffectionate housekeeper. This odd background gives Lyra another strong advantage as a storybook heroine. Child heroes who possess loving parents always face a problem in fiction. If they play everything safe, as any properly concerned parent would wish them to, their capacity for adventure is going to be strictly limited. If on the other hand they go in for dangerous exploits, this will mean going against what all good parents would wish for their child. Deliberately running terrible risks is less easy to contemplate with parents who are affectionate, concerned and therefore deserving of trust. But disobeying bad parents, or harsh parent-substitutes, is not a matter for guilt. Accordingly, Lyra stays guilt-free on this issue, given that she does not even know at the start of her story that she has parents who are still living.

When she discovers that they are Mrs Coulter and Lord Asriel, she has even less reason to consider the wishes of such an unpleasant and selfish pair. Having grown up as an orphan, she comes over as someone who has largely invented herself, and who still retains the possibility of reinventing herself once again should the occasion demand. Fictional children possessing caring, hands-on parents can never aspire to the same level of independence, which from the start makes Lyra such a potentially interesting as well as attractive character.

She sees her extended family instead as the street urchins, college servants and remote scholars all of whom have taken some loose part in bringing her up. Particular friends like Roger, the Jordan College kitchen boy, play an extra significant part in her life given that she has no other close ties. This helps explain why, in *The Amber Spyglass*, it is so important for Lyra to rescue Roger from the land of the dead. The loyalty she feels towards him is similar to how a sister might react when a beloved brother is killed, partly – as she believes – through her own fault.

At other moments, Lyra feels strongly for a succession of father and mother figures, each one providing the sort of parental love and concern that she has never experienced at first hand. John Faa the Gyptian leader, Iorek Byrnison the armoured bear, Lee Scoresby the aviator, Serafina Pekkala the witch and Mary Malone, the nun-turned-research-scientist, all at some stage perform a role in Lyra's life that would have been more appropriately played by a mother and father. Once again, there are distinct storytelling advantages here. A succession of different, interesting and sometimes bizarre parent-figures is always going to make for more intriguing characters than one pair of ordinarily well-intentioned parents.

As the only girl on John Faa's boat expedition to the North, Lyra soon makes herself busy in the manner of another of Pullman's favourite characters in fiction. This is Tim, the tough small boy in Edward Ardizzone's famous picture book *Little Tim and the Brave Sea Captain* and its various successors. After stowing away on a small boat, Tim is set to work and quickly makes the best of things, even when he seems to be facing certain death. Lyra is also soon on friendly relations with the rest of the crew, and like Tim is allowed to work the ship's steam whistle and help the cook with his plum duff.

This combination of ordinary naughtiness and extreme responsibility under pressure makes her a splendidly well-rounded character, neither oppressively good nor monotonously rebellious. She has those human faults all readers can identify with as well as other virtues that they can freely admire. Nicknamed Silvertongue at one stage, she is also a natural storyteller.

But when Lyra tries to get the better of the harpies by telling them a pack of worthless lies, their indignant screams of 'Liar! Liar!' show her that this policy will never work. The whole episode is a reminder that Lyra's very name, with its overtones of lyre – the instrument of the gods – can also be heard as 'liar' as well. She realises from that moment on that only stories concerned with what she knows to be the truth are going to do. Such stories must draw on her knowledge of what it is really like to be alive, aiming to get everything exactly right as she sees and feels it. In that sense, Lyra stands for the author himself, and his corresponding efforts to get at what he sees as the genuine truth in his imaginative vision of the world, however much this might offend various interested parties along the way.

When interviewed Pullman insists that Lyra is in fact a very ordinary child, and that he had met thousands like her when he was a teacher. As he puts it in the first story of the trilogy: 'She was a coarse and greedy little savage, for the most part.' But he also adds elsewhere that: 'The point I am making is that ordinary people are capable of great deeds.' Lyra finally comes through because Pullman believes that all humans have the capacity to be heroic, given the right circumstances. Many would find this an overoptimistic opinion, with Lyra obviously something special by virtue of her outsize courage, superb sense of loyalty and general toughness under fire. But Pullman takes a positive line about human potential wherever it is found. His belief that people can always make the best of their own lives if only they are left alone by religion, or any other authoritarian system of thought, is central to his philosophy.

Although he is the same age, Will is a sadder and more solemn character than Lyra. He has had to shoulder the experience of the loss of his father as well as take responsibility for his mentally ill mother. When others torment her, it is Will who protects her, while also trying to cope with his own bruised and angry feelings. Although having already accidentally killed a man is a major worry to him, he still seems drawn to violence. He says at one time to Lyra: 'I got my own things to do in Oxford, and if you give me away, I'll kill you.' As he has previously told her that he is a murderer, she has no reason to disbelieve him.

Without his own visible dæmon for emotional support, Will remains a rather closed personality for most of the trilogy, much in need of more mothering himself. Silent, sometimes moody, but strong and determined when he needs to be, he makes a splendid romantic hero of the old school. It takes his growing feelings for Lyra to give him the confidence to talk about his past unhappiness. When he finally realises that he loves Lyra, he becomes a whole person at last, able to admit to the strong feelings he had up till then kept hidden away. He also by now has the maturity to destroy the knife with which he could have mastered the world.

He does this because he realises that although his own intentions about the possible future uses of the knife are worthy ones, the knife itself has its own plans too, and cannot of itself be trusted. So Will finally breaks it by bringing to mind the one thing it is unable to cut: his love for Lyra. The previous time the knife broke happened when Mrs Coulter filled Will's mind with the image of his much-loved mother. But Will is moving on now in his own maturity, and it is fitting that his love for Lyra now seems to him the most urgent sensation in his life.

He and Lyra both have troubled relationships with their own parents, in one case because there is not enough love and in the other because there may be too much. Resolving their individual psychological needs is something else Will and Lyra have to do on their own, coming out stronger in the end though not before moments of pain. But until they can manage to solve their personal problems they are powerless to see to their most important task, which is nothing less than the saving of the world. The necessity for learning to look both forwards and outwards is another important message in this book, which has little time for those continually trapped in a past that prevents them from enjoying the joys, wonders and duties of the world they are living in at the present.

Fantasies about particular chosen leaders do not always end on a positive note; the mythological leader and saviour King Arthur, for example, dies before his time as part of his destiny. If Pullman's trilogy also ended abruptly in tragedy, it is doubtful whether it would have enjoyed anything like the same success. But although Lyra and Will often suffer, both during their stories and at the moment of their final sever-ance, the whole trilogy is fundamentally about the triumph of good actions over evil ones. This is never a victory that can be taken for granted. As Dr Lanselius says of Lyra, taking his cue from the prophecies made by the witches about her for centuries past: 'she must be free to make mistakes. We must hope that she does not, but we can't guide her.'

As the most important chosen instrument of good, Lyra

comes over as an ideal character with whom readers can identify. Sometimes contrary over small details, she is magnificently brave when it really matters. Long realising that she has been picked out to do a special task, however much others believe that she is still ignorant of what her destiny demands of her, she never flinches from this duty. But Lyra has to wait until she finally knows what it is she has to do – which in her case, is to abolish death itself by liberating all those ghosts currently wasting away in a grim underworld.

Will also has his destiny marked out for him, and like Lyra also possesses freedom of choice. As he explains to his father at the end of the trilogy, 'You said I was a warrior. You told me that was my nature, and I shouldn't argue with it. Father, you were wrong. I fought because I had to. I can't choose my nature, but I can choose what I do. And I *will* choose, because now I'm free.'

There is always a problem, however, over freedom of choice with characters who seem to be fulfilling the various prophecies previously made about them. This issue of free will versus destiny is also central to one of Pullman's key influences, Milton's *Paradise Lost*, given that an all-knowing, all-powerful God should surely by definition always have been able to intervene in order to save Adam and Eve from committing their sin in the first place. But Pullman overcomes this problem by making both Will and Lyra such independent characters that it is impossible to imagine them ever doing anything simply because someone else has told them that they either should or will. What drives them is their sense of what should be, according to their own values and personalities.

This is an important point for both characters, since if they were simply doing what they were always required to do by the greater forces pushing them along they would be little better than robots. But it is not just heroes who must have the power of choice in order to qualify as such. All human beings have to make important choices throughout their lives, and the better they choose, the better it will ultimately be – not just for themselves but also for others. Will and Lyra set an example whereby, whatever the opposition, they insist on making a stand for what they believe to be right. If more people acted in a similar way, the story implies, our own world might be in a much healthier state.

Young people often have a similar fantasy at some stage that they too are extra special, selected by some mysterious force one day to astonish the world. This particular myth of the self frequently lingers on into adulthood, before accumulated experience finally proves to at least most of us that we really are very much like everyone else after all. In Lyra and Will, readers of all ages can identify with young heroes for whom this fantasy is a living reality. No wonder that so many took to them so quickly, with their story stirring up similarly flattering fantasies of the type that have always persisted deep in the spirit of all human beings.

His Dark Materials was published at the same time as J.K. Rowling's *Harry Potter* stories. Both writers had experience of losing a parent when they were still children and both have since admitted to periods of depression in their lives, symbolised by attacks from the Spectres in Pullman's stories and similar assaults by the Dementors in Rowling's novels. Both have had to come to terms with adversity, Rowling as a single mother trying to get by in poverty and Pullman, disappointed after his poor Oxford degree, casting around for an occupation when all he wanted to do was write. It is perhaps no coincidence that both writers have created young characters who have had to battle against the odds for some time before achieving their ends.

Lyra, Will and Harry also come from troubled homes, where there has either been a marked absence of love or else a parent who was not coping. All have been chosen by some unknown force to carry out a great deed that will save the world. All are equal to this task because of their innate courage and moral integrity, and each one possesses an exceptional gift: Harry with his powers of magic, Lyra with her alethiometer and Will with his knife.

They also receive important help from friends but little or nothing from parents or parent-substitutes. Harry is an orphan, Lyra starts by thinking she is one, and Will has never known his father. All are, to this extent, self-created characters, responsible primarily to themselves for want of any parent or parent figure to take responsibility for them. All share the traditional attributes of the fictional lone hero, born in unusual circumstances but with access to extraordinary powers. All too are early on linked to a prophecy that marks them out as key figures in the saving of their own society.

Characters found in today's children's or Young Adult novels are not always so perfect. This is because modern fiction, whether for adults or children, often prefers to go in the direction of psychological realism when describing main characters, avoiding heroics in favour of revealing human flaws as well as strengths. Main characters are often shown as only coming into their own once they have defeated their various personal weaknesses on the way. Others are admired for the way they get the better of severe personal or social disadvantages.

But Lyra, Will and Harry seem to have been born both strong and good. While other children might have become severely disturbed by the sort of childhood all three endured, they come across as oblivious to every bad influence that might have had a negative effect upon them. The problems they have to defeat come from outside and rarely from their own personalities. Together they signal a return to a simpler fictional world whose heroes nearly always do the right thing. They also, through their courage, humanity and high sense of morality, represent exemplars of the perpetual human need for undoubted heroes or heroines, if only in the imagination.

Best-selling writers inevitably reflect some of the most popular feelings and fantasies of their own times, and such too could be the case with the creation of Lyra, Will and Harry. In a modern age where biographers, satirists and journalists are eager to cut down anyone who might otherwise seem to be setting a reasonably good or possibly even a heroic example, Lyra, Will and Harry offer a welcome contrast. They are shown throughout to be independent, largely insulated from social influences and very much their own creations. While other characters in their stories are unequal to the mighty task of putting the world to rights, they somehow have the key. Many readers looking at their own world could be forgiven for wishing – at least in their dreams – that similarly wise and brave heroes could one day also sort out some of the most dangerous political and social problems that exist in real life.

Supporters of genetic engineering have sometimes insisted that they may soon have the techniques to produce babies who are healthy and intelligent as never before. The whole idea of producing superior human beings, whether through genetic engineering or any other process, is of course another fantasy in its own right. Pullman's and Rowling's literary fantasies are of a quite different order, but there may still be some common ground here. Scientists who believe they can one day produce a better type of person and novelists who actually write about such beings are both to an extent reacting to a current dissatisfaction with humans as they actually are and the mess they are making of the world we all live in. A general lack of confidence over the future suggests that there is at present little conviction that things will improve unless human beings themselves change for the better. With no evidence that this will ever happen, it is not surprising that stories about such super-humans, young or old, continue to attract readers of all ages.

There are many other ways in which these stories appeal so powerfully to readers, and in particular to children. All the books in which these characters appear follow a pattern whereby good finally defeats evil in a cosmic battle whose opposing sides are, with some exceptions, clearly drawn. Lyra, Will and Harry do not just represent the best type of person. They also perform valiantly in the service of a moral goodness always clearly visible to them, however difficult it might sometimes be to discern in ordinary daily life, well away from the world of storytelling.

Science and Religion

Knowing your enemy:
Lyra and Will versus the Church

E arly on in *Northern Lights* the alethiometer reveals that Lyra is going to play an important part in a major battle. This starts as a dispute between the Holy Church and her own father Lord Asriel, over the possible existence of other worlds beyond the present one and the conventional Christian view of only one other spiritual world in existence made up of heaven and hell. Later on this turns into a fight to the death between those who support further enslavement by evil Church forces versus those who want final liberation from spiritual oppression from whatever source.

This story can also be read as a fable, with Lyra and Will standing in for Adam and Eve. The suggestion is that our own cultural history might have developed along healthier lines had the story of the Garden of Eden been interpreted in the first place with Eve the heroine rather than the villain of the piece. Far from an act of tragic disobedience, Pullman clearly believes that her decision to eat the apple from the tree of knowledge was the right thing to do.

All the disgrace visited upon this action since stems in his view from the Church's determination to keep everyone in a state of continual guilt and fear. Congregations brought up to feel like this are then all the more willing to turn towards an organised religion that promises redemption for the first great, human sin that Pullman believes should never have been described as such. Now, in a re-run of this famous story, Lyra and Will also disobey the teachings of the Church, but are seen by their supporters to have done the right thing, not just for themselves but for everyone else as well.

Lyra starts out in the trilogy as a child, but finishes with the experience of a first, passionate love affair. As Mrs Coulter puts it to the evil President of the Consistorial Court: 'My daughter is now twelve years old. Very soon she will approach the cusp of adolescence, and then it will be too late for any of us to prevent the catastrophe; nature and opportunity will come together like spark and tinder.'

As so often, Mrs Coulter is playing a double game here, and in the next moment she turns against the Church, describing the whole court as 'a body of men with a feverish obsession with sexuality, men with dirty fingernails, reeking of ancient sweat, men whose furtive imaginations would crawl over [Lyra's] body like cockroaches'. But there is no doubt that the court sees Lyra's progress towards taking up a positive attitude about her own sexuality as a severe threat. Should she, like Eve before her, also give way to what the Church defines as temptation but which Lyra would experience as love without guilt, this will surely ruin the authority of the whole ecclesiastical establishment. That is why its president, Father MacPhail, proposes to send out someone to kill her.

Pullman also suggests that the overwhelming sense of shame described in the Bible after Adam and Eve became aware of their naked sexuality for the first time, far from being a natural outcome, was actually imposed upon them by the grim-faced Authority. This action then allowed him a perfect method of control over them and subsequently everyone else. Since all humans coming after would inevitably develop sexual awareness, being taught to feel bad about such feelings allowed the Authority, now naming himself as God, a perfect method of control ever after. Having imposed a seal of shame on all believers, the Church could then set itself up as the only institution capable of bestowing forgiveness for a state of consciousness that in fact never needed to be excused or forgiven in the first place.

But if Lyra, as a modern Eve, discovers that her first consciousness of sexuality is a joyful and loving process, then the former power of the Church to impose guilt and fear in this area could be lost forever. Exactly how Lyra's example would filter through to everyone else is never made clear. But everyone in the trilogy knows how important Lyra is and how long her presence has been prophesied. The ultimate positive effect she will have on her own society if she wins through must simply be taken for granted.

Pullman's attack on Christianity takes off in other directions. He is not against the idea of one great force in the universe, of the type that makes the northern lights glow and may be pushing the hands of the alethiometer at the same time. But he hates all the attempts by human agencies to first claim this force for themselves and then use it for evil purposes. In this trilogy, God, or the Authority, is simply the first angel to be 'condensed out of Dust'. He told all the angels that came after him that he was their creator, but this was not true.

At the end of the trilogy, this figure is revealed to Mrs Coulter as nothing more than an anguished, aged being, 'of terrifying decrepitude, of a face sunken in wrinkles, of trembling hands and a mumbling mouth and rheumy eyes'. Demented and powerless, he finally dissolves in the wind after Lyra and Will help him out of his crystal litter. He does so with 'a sigh of the most profound and exhausted relief'. His Regent, Metatron, who had long been running things, is the Biblical figure Enoch, a direct descendant of Adam. He too is anxious for power and ruthless about how he gets it. In this he is well served on earth by the Church, which uses the original lies of the Authority to back up its own claims for power over other fellow humans.

This ultra-negative view of Christianity and the Church could seem strange now, at a time when, at least in most parts of the Western world, religious belief is generally on the wane. But Pullman is having nothing of this. In his lecture on the Republic of Heaven, given in 2000, he writes: 'of all the dangers that threaten us at the beginning of the third millennium – the degradation of the environment, the increasingly undemocratic power of the great corporations, the continuing threats to peace in regions full of decaying nuclear weapons, and so on – one of the biggest dangers of all comes from fundamentalist religion.' He goes on to pick out in particular the threat posed at the time by Christian conservatives in the USA and the Taliban in Afghanistan.

One of the arguments for any organised religion has always been that humans need a fixed code of conduct without which they may be too weak to conduct their lives for the best. Pullman rejects this case on both counts. He does not think that the code of conduct suggested by Christianity is always either good or humane, and he believes that humans have it within themselves to live happy, fulfilled lives without encouragement or threats from religion. But as he has admitted himself: 'There is a depressing human tendency to say "We know the truth and we're going to kill you because you don't believe in it."' Why so many human beings should have lent themselves to attitudes like this both in the past

14. A watercolour painting from William Blake's *Book of Urizen*:
'The Immortal endur'd his chains, / Tho' bound in a deadly
sleep.' Blake has been a particular hero of and influence on
Pullman. (*The Book of Urizen* (1794), plate 22, copy G, c.1815.
Reproduced by permission of the Library of Congress.)

and present, and what this means for Pullman's more hopeful view about humanity, is a matter his novels have yet to come to terms with.

As far as Western Europe is concerned, Pullman's reasons for his passionate dislike of Christianity in the trilogy sometimes belong to things that happened in the remote past. He twice mentions the fact that John Calvin, the seventeenth-century Protestant reformer based in Geneva, occasionally ordered the deaths of those children he believed to be heretics. Elsewhere, the witch Serafina Pekkala warns her sisters that there are modern churches that cut children's sexual organs 'with knives so that they shan't feel'. But if this is a reference to female genital mutilation, this is something that Christian forces in Africa have long been condemning.

Pullman gives a clue to what he is getting at here when Lord Asriel lectures Lyra about the Church's tradition of cutting children:

Do you know what the word *castration* means? It means removing the sexual organs of a boy so that he never develops the characteristics of a man. A *castrato* keeps his high treble voice all his life, which is why the Church allowed it: so useful in Church music. Some *castrati* became great singers, wonderful artists. Many just became fat spoiled half-men. Some died from the effects of the operation. But the Church wouldn't flinch at the idea of a little *cut*, you see.

This loathsome practice is not found in any Christian religion today, and was once widespread in many different cultures. So once again, it seems hard to blame it on Christianity alone. The various priest characters in the trilogy, whether they enjoy vodka too much, watch over acts of torture or set out to commit murder, also come over as uniformly nasty. Like the caricatures found in the atheistic propaganda put over in pre-war Soviet Russia, these characters suggest that a good clergyman or nun has never existed. This is clearly unfair, as is the suggestion in the trilogy that the Church is only concerned with its own cruel and cynical survival, and is happy to kidnap, torture and murder to that end.

Pullman believes that 'Every single religion that has a monotheistic god ends up by persecuting other people and killing them because they don't accept him. Wherever you look in history you find that. It's still going on.' But since he knows the Christian religion best, this is where he pitches his main attack. For him, Christianity is a powerful and convincing force that has adversely shaped Western culture ever since it was first adopted. In this view, the Christian concept of the Kingdom of Heaven has always been an authoritarian attempt to impose negative values on populations, backed up by the weight of a self-serving Church hierarchy.

The end result, for him, has been the inevitable persecution of all those who oppose this system of belief. Such persecution is certainly less obvious now than it has been in the past, but in terms of the trilogy, Lyra's world of Brytain is different in many ways from Will's up-to-date version of Britain today. If the powers of the Church in Lyra's life have developed in new and horrible directions this, in Pullman's view, is because the seeds of this type of religious tyranny have always been implicit in Christianity anyway. While such tyranny is relatively restrained in Will's world, it is running out of control in Lyra's Brytain, just as it sometimes has in our own past.

What Pullman argues for instead is the reverse ideal of a Republic of Heaven, inhabited by people who have been brought up to value both themselves and others. In this scenario, the guilt and shame about sex encouraged by the Bible would be replaced by an honest admission of the joys and pleasures of the body. Instead of turning to priests and the Bible for advice, people instead should learn to trust their own instincts to do the right thing. The aim should always be to live harmoniously with themselves and with each other in an environment that is also loved and protected. Far from condemning Eve for eating from the tree of knowledge, Pullman believes that she should be seen as heroic in her determination to find out things for herself – the basis for all true education.

As for the powers of the Church as they appear in his

trilogy, it is clear that Pullman is not only aiming at oppressive religion in his description of the various forces of darkness threatening to take over every world wherever they exist. He is also attacking all authoritarian systems of thought, religious or otherwise, that set out to enslave their followers under the guise of caring for them. As John Parry puts it to his son: 'Every little increase in human freedom has been fought over ferociously between those who want us to know more and be wiser and stronger, and those who want us to obey and be humble and submit.'

Some would argue that there are times in history as well as in the contemporary world when this apparently clear division between good and bad is not as easy to make out. But in broad terms at least, this overall view enables Pullman to attack many other villains in addition to oppressive religion in his trilogy. The cruelty inflicted on the kidnapped children when their dæmons are cut away is more reminiscent of some of the abominable experiments carried out in Nazi concentration camps than anything to do with the modern Church.

The spiritual starvation and environmental degradation that so often go together in dictatorships also occur in the various descriptions of lost, cowed societies found in the trilogy. Lyra does not therefore just stand for spiritual freedom; she also represents the physical and social freedom that should be the aim of any truly civilised country for its citizens, young or old. This is not an argument for anarchy, given that

Pullman also provides plenty of examples where individuals act with a just authority that deserves to be obeyed, from Iorek the bear to Dame Hannah, the wise head teacher who takes on Lyra as her pupil at the end of the trilogy. But such authority must be earned rather than assumed, and it should always act with a strong sense of responsibility.

Parallel worlds

Lyra and Will live in parallel worlds, resembling each other in some ways but different in others. In the course of their travels, they enter other worlds as well. This may seem a strange direction to take for a writer so intent on the idea of making the best of the here and now in his fiction, yet there are good reasons for this plot device. Pullman takes his cue here from modern quantum theory, which challenges former truths once held to be standard with the idea of uncertainty as a built-in factor to all science.

This has led distinguished physicists such as David Deutsch to claim that the results of certain 'double slit' experiments with light constitute evidence for the existence of parallel worlds. This claim has been disputed, but the main argument, once unthinkable where orthodox scientific reasoning is concerned, still has its followers. The Palmerian Professor at Jordan College refers it to when he mentions 'the Barnard-Stokes business' to Lord Asriel at the start of *Northern Lights*. Later on, the Master of Jordan explains to the librarian how these two daring theologians had postulated 'the existence of numerous other worlds like this one, neither heaven nor hell, but material and sinful'.

The basic premise about the possible existence of parallel universes arises from what might happen should one particular action have two possible results at the same moment. Let Pullman explain the main idea behind this for himself, talking through the pursed lips of Lord Asriel:

> Take the example of tossing a coin: it can come down heads or tails, and we don't know before it lands which way it's going to fall. If it comes down heads, that means that the possibility of its coming down tails has collapsed. Until that moment the two possibilities were equal.
>
> But on another world, it does come down tails. And when that happens, the two worlds split apart. I'm using the example of tossing a coin to make it clearer. In fact, these possibility-collapses happen at the level of elementary particles, but they happen in just the same way: one moment several things are possible, the next moment only one happens, and the rest don't exist. Except that other worlds have sprung into being, on which they *did* happen.

Pullman puts this idea of other worlds to maximum use in his trilogy, showing readers how each of the societies that he describes has gone on to grow in its own particular style. The same is true of individual development. While sitting together on a moss-covered rock, Will and Lyra reflect on 'how many tiny chances had conspired to bring them to this place. Each of those chances might have gone a different way'. The overall message is that because nothing that happens is ever inevitable, it is up to the people that live in whichever world – including our own – always to make the best of the various opportunities that come their way.

At a plot level, parallel universes also have advantages, allowing Pullman to use his gift for describing other worlds that are a fascinating mixture of the strange and the familiar. Some of these details of daily life in other worlds are drawn not just from the present but also from the nineteenth century, such as the naphtha lights and zeppelins that crop up throughout the trilogy. Others are entirely imaginary, like the alethiometer, a device for reading the future taking its name from *aletheia*, the Greek word for truth, or the various dæmons that accompany people in Lyra's world. In all cases, the effect is to keep the reader in a state of imaginative wonder – for Pullman, one of the principal aims of all fiction.

What is Dust?

Pullman never actually states who or what he thinks does actually run the universe, and for good reason. To do so would be to run into exactly the same trap that has snared everyone else attempting to narrow down and specify a power that he believes remains impossible to understand, however clearly it is sometimes felt. At one moment Serafina Pekkala tells Lee Scoresby of Lyra that 'it seems that the fates are using her as a messenger to take [the alethiometer] to her father'. Later on Jotham Santelia, Professor of Cosmology, assures Lyra that: 'The stars are alive, child. Did you know that? Everything out there is alive, and there are grand purposes abroad! ... Everything happens for a purpose.'

It is a short step from this position to move on to the idea that the elementary particles that make up life may themselves also possess consciousness, just as they do in the Dust that plays such an important part in all three stories. Pullman takes his own particular use of this word straight from a verse in the Bible. When God is cursing Adam for having eaten the forbidden fruit, he tells him: 'For dust thou art, and unto dust shalt thou return.'

As Lord Asriel explains to Lyra, some scholars believe this should actually be translated as 'Thou shalt be subject to dust'. But for Pullman, Dust has many different meanings. He defines it variously throughout the trilogy as original sin, the form of thoughts not yet born, dark matter, shadow-particles,

particles of consciousness and even as rebel angels. This cosmic Dust is distributed throughout space and is at one with the universe itself. Death is described as a joyful process of re-integration with Dust rather than with any Christian idea of God. This belief is not far from the eighteenth-century idea of pantheism, whereby God is seen as everything and everything is seen as God.

Pantheism is in fact a very ancient belief, far older than Christianity, and forms the basis for many other world religions still in existence today. At its heart is a reverence for the whole universe as well as for the native earth, seen as something sacred. Supernatural gods play no part in this religion. Animal as well as human rights are respected, and there is a commitment never to harm the natural environment. Humans themselves are held to be made of the same matter as the universe, and only in this life do they have the chance to witness this earthly paradise face to face. When they die, they are reunited with nature by being re-absorbed into it. But should they destroy nature, they then risk creating a hell on earth for all species as well as for themselves.

Pullman's notion of Dust may therefore also have links with a particular mystical-ecological approach to the earth. In this view the world – like Dust – has always been a living organism with its own needs and feelings. The Greeks recognised this by giving the earth its own individual name of Gaia, the Greek name for the Goddess who was the original earth-mother. Humankind that so freely pollutes the world continues to neglect this mighty living organism at its own extreme peril.

His Dark Materials is packed with examples of environmental devastation, running hand in hand with descriptions of accompanying human cruelty, neglect and intolerance. For Pullman, bad behaviour towards other humans is inseparable from behaving badly towards the living environment. In both cases, violence is shattering what should be a natural harmony and still could be, if only humans learned how to act in ways where 'responsibility and delight can co-exist'. In this, they could well afford to follow the example of the gentle, inoffensive mulefa, who work *with*, rather than against, their environment. By using giant seed-pods as wheels to help them travel, they also bring these same pods to a state where they finally crack after so much pounding along hard roads. After that, it is possible for the mulefa to extract the seeds which are then tended carefully as they grow into new plants.

Dust may also be linked to superstring theory found in the discussion of quantum physics today. Sometimes also known as the Theory of Everything, this states that at the most microscopic level everything in the universe is made up of loops of vibrating strings. An object such as an apple, and a force such as radiation, can in this theory both be broken down into atoms, which can then be further broken down into electrons and quarks. These in turn can finally be reduced to tiny, vibrating loops of string.

This essential indivisibility of matter and energy could help explain why Pullman has endowed Dust with consciousness as well as an only barely visible physical shape. As Mary Malone discovers, it made its presence felt in human evolution partly in order to extract vengeance. This was for the betrayal of humanity that occurred when the rebel angels lost the great battle that once raged in heaven. These angels were also composed of Dust. At other times this precious shadow-matter can only be approached obliquely. When Lyra turns to the alethiometer, or Will makes use of his knife, it is important that they stay in a relaxed, totally open and receptive state of mind, putting their own immediate thoughts to one side.

Yet if humans can never confront Dust directly, they can still become conscious of examples of its essential truth. The better any of us live, Pullman says, the more likely that we too might experience the type of positive joy that also drives the entire world. Cruelty, greed and selfishness, on the other hand, only obscure what is good and true. When these negative impulses become linked to evil political or religious movements, the results can be disastrous. Dust, of itself, has no power to shape human lives. Only we can do that; but by doing the best we can we will, in Pullman's view, then be working in the true spirit of this special Dust rather than against it.

This is not to say that Dust in itself, when we finally return to it, offers a necessarily better alternative to life on earth.

When Serafina Pekkala watches the gleaming angels flying away, she feels nothing but compassion for these magnificent beings composed only of light and Dust: 'How much they must miss, never to feel the earth beneath their feet, or the wind in their hair, or the tingle of the starlight on their bare skin!'

Later on, Mrs Coulter makes the important discovery about angels that 'lacking flesh, they coveted it and longed for contact with it'. For Pullman, therefore, it is still best to be human, enjoying all the legitimate pleasures of the body that we have been blessed with but which religion in the past has sometimes condemned so cruelly. As Will explains to Lyra: 'Angels wish they had bodies. They told me that angels can't understand why *we* don't enjoy the world more. It would be [a] sort of ecstasy for them to have our flesh and our senses.'

He is not simply referring to sexuality here. Pullman is an enthusiast for all types of physical joy, there to be relished without the shame and guilt that religion has sometimes tried to attach to any sort of sensual enjoyment in life. A good example of this belief occurs at the moment when Mary Malone feels she is somehow being carried away from her own body and desperately attempts to fight back:

She flung a mental lifeline to that physical self, and tried to recall the feeling of being in it: all the sensations that made up being alive [...] The taste of bacon and eggs. The triumphant strain in her muscles as she pulled herself up a rockface. The delicate dancing of her fingers on a computer keyboard. The smell of roasting coffee. The warmth of her bed on a winter night.

Mary survives this episode; Pullman makes it clear that this is supremely well worth it, given that now she possesses the capacity to find delight in comparatively simple pleasures. But those children cut away from their dæmons before reaching adolescence will never get to experience such strong feelings in any areas of their lives. Mrs Coulter tries to explain the positive side of this whole, cruel practice of intercision to an unconvinced Lyra: 'All that happens is a little cut, and then everything's peaceful. For ever! You see, your dæmon's a wonderful friend and companion when you're young, but at the age we call puberty […] dæmons bring all sorts of troublesome thoughts and feelings, and that's what lets Dust in.'

Losing a dæmon, therefore, is akin to losing an individual's adult soul. Without it, there can be no contact with that vital Dust that is also synonymous with energy, consciousness and freedom of thought. Like the victims of the Spectres, those without dæmons become 'indifferent [and] dead in life'. But with their own dæmons and therefore remaining open to attracting Dust as adults, individuals are able to become fully formed human beings, conscious of their own potential and able to make informed decisions about the rest of their lives.

So who or what is in ultimate control of everything? What force, for example, both powers and informs the alethiometer?

Who exactly picked out Lyra for her great task of saving the world, and who originally prophesied that it would be a girl who would be the chosen saviour? Pullman offers no clear answers here, nor does he wish to. He disapproves of systems of thought such as organised religion that attempt to explain and account for everything within the world and the spirit. His own belief system is basically intuitive rather than worked out to the last letter.

Dæmons

Lyra's dæmon is named Pantalaimon, which means 'all merciful' in Greek. The word 'dæmon' also derives from the Greek, with Socrates at one stage talking about his own *daimon*, which in his terms was a cross between a conscience and a guardian angel. Always addressed as Pan, Lyra's dæmon is a visible personal soul or spirit, able to take on any animal form. Everyone in Lyra's world has his or her own dæmon, whose shape only becomes constant once an individual has grown beyond childhood into late adolescence. Such dæmons act variously as confidants, advisers, spies, look-outs, defenders, occasional scolds, best-loved intimates and, most especially, the voice of conscience.

They are particularly important in this story where Lyra is concerned. As a child with an absent, neglectful mother and a father who is almost as bad, Lyra has the type of childhood that in normal circumstances would be described as severely deprived. Although the tutors at Jordan College take an absent-minded interest in her, there is no one who clearly loves her and whom she can love in return – except, of course, for her dæmon.

Pan therefore has a vital role in this story. Like nearly all dæmons, he is of the opposite sex to his human counterpart. As such, he corresponds to the psychologist Carl Jung's idea that all humans have a craving for another half, also of the opposite sex which, if we could reunite with it, would then mean that we could at last become truly whole individuals. This concept is described in Jungian terms as the lifelong search for the *anima*, where men are concerned, and the *animus* in the case of women. But because we can never be joined up to our missing male or female counterparts, Jung believes we must always go through life with the feeling that there is something important missing within us.

Lyra has no such problems, since her dæmon already gives her all the love and support she needs. This is vital for the plot, since it would otherwise be difficult even to start believing that a ten-year-old girl on her own could be equal to any of the acts of daring and courage that Lyra manages to carry off throughout this story. In real life, a child as deprived as she is could well have major and sometimes disabling psychological problems to deal with long before getting to the fearful adventures she triumphs over in this story.

But with her own dæmon as constant support and always ready with a friendly word or understanding look, Lyra can take on any of the tasks at hand. Readers, in their turn, are offered an exceptionally pleasing fantasy of the type that has always been popular in children's fiction, with its long tradition of describing heroes who also possess ideal companions. From the story of Dick Whittington's cat to modern classics like Clive King's *Stig of the Dump* and Raymond Briggs's *The Snowman*, the idea of the main character blessed with a close and beloved friend has been a constant theme. Hamlet has always needed his Horatio, Don Quixote could never manage without his patient servant Sancho Panza, and Sherlock Holmes would not have had half as satisfying a time without his great friend Dr Watson.

But more recently in teenage fiction, there seems to have been less emphasis upon the role of the special friend. There are several reasons why fiction may be following contemporary trends in this respect. Many of today's teenagers now expect to develop romantically-oriented relationships with the opposite sex far earlier than was once the case, leaving less time for more ordinary, less intense same-sex friendships. The time that proper friendship requires in order to get established is more limited now in other ways, with ever-more-demanding schoolwork during term-time and holiday jobs in the vacations. Allowing their children to spend a lot of time away from home, with or without friends, is also less popular with parents now, anxious that something bad may happen when they are not there.

Many fictional best friends still exist in teenage books, but even here those that there are can occasionally turn into a worst enemy. This happens in Anne Fine's memorable novel *The Tulip Touch*, and there are other stories where friendship causes as many problems as it once seemed to solve. Against this background, the idea of a personal dæmon offers all the consolations of the closest and most intense friendship, without any of the possible disadvantages. The British psychotherapist Donald Winnicott once wrote that every individual has the need to create what he called a 'caretaker self'. This is that internal voice that tries to cheer up someone, particularly when he or she is down, acting as a sympathetic and reassuring friend at all times.

In this sense, dæmons too can surely claim to be caretaker selves of a different order. Always on the side of their human counterpart, they can actually be seen and heard, as well as felt. Will can't wait to see his dæmon, who has hitherto always been invisible to him. When she finally flies down, 'he felt his heart tighten and release in a way he never forgot'. And so, to the great love between Will and Lyra that serves as the final climax of the trilogy can also be added the equally profound love they have for their respective dæmons. Both of these loving and intimate relationships – to each other as well as to their dæmons – represent an ideal to which humans have constantly aspired.

Realistic novels for young readers commonly stress the pain experienced by those children suffering from adverse social or psychological conditions. Readers afterwards may also find themselves more alert to the various signs of mental or physical stress in other children who are going through a particularly difficult time in real life. But fantasy stories, including this trilogy, often have a quite different sort of agenda. They may be more concerned with extending the imaginative world into the realms of the truly extraordinary, making use of main characters able to survive everything thrown at them precisely because they do not have the weaknesses and problems common in real life.

But there may still be issues of credibility here, even in a fantasy story, when it comes to making such bold adventurers believable at the same time. So giving Lyra the additional backing of her own personalised dæmon is one brilliant way of effectively winning readers over to the idea that she really could always behave in the courageous and independent way that she does. It also enables Pullman to turn what would normally be private thoughts into an ongoing dialogue, given that Lyra and her dæmon constantly talk to and argue with each other throughout their story. This is particularly true in moments of stress when it comes to deciding what to do next.

Lord Asriel and Mrs Coulter

L ord Asriel is Lyra's unloving, superior and short-tempered father. Is he on the side of good and Dust or is he simply playing his own selfish game? Like Satan in Milton's *Paradise Lost*, he is a mixture of both good and bad. His mighty ambition is to destroy God himself, just as Milton's Satan wants to wage a war in order to regain a place in heaven after his expulsion for rebelling against God. But after more thought, Satan decides to investigate new worlds instead, just as Lord Asriel does. Like Satan, by building a bridge to another world Lord Asriel risks upsetting the natural order, and in so doing may have been instrumental in introducing the plague of Spectres unleashed on the world. It is for this type of reason that the otherwise kindly Master of Jordan College tries to poison him early on, conscious that if his bold scientific investigations into other worlds were allowed to continue they could eventually bring disaster for all.

Although Milton describes him as evil and malicious, readers often find something heroic in the depiction of Satan, and the terrible energy that goes into his quest for power and revenge. As William Blake put it: 'The reason Milton wrote in fetters when he wrote of angels and heaven, and at liberty when he wrote of devils and hell, is that he was a true poet and of the devil's party without knowing it.' Lord Asriel too is a more vivid, colourful figure than some of the more anodyne angel characters that crop up in Pullman's books. When he appears, things happen, however unpleasantly he may behave in the process.

Lord Asriel finally dies to save his daughter Lyra. He is also determined to protect Dust from its many enemies, and fights bravely in the various pitched battles that result from doing this. So on this basis, both Satan and Lord Asriel could be seen to be on the side of essential human freedom. While Satan battled in vain against what Pullman sees as a jealous and restrictive God, Lord Asriel takes up the fight against the evils of organised religion that in this account plague humankind.

Milton's Satan suffered from a sinful pride that constantly led him to make bad decisions. The same too is true of Lord Asriel. Cold and rejecting towards his daughter, he is willing to sacrifice the life of a child in order to further his attempts to travel to another world. He revels in his scientific power not just for what it can achieve but also for its own sake. When he boasts to Mrs Coulter that 'You and I could take the universe to pieces and put it together again', there seems little doubt that he is beginning to think that he is something like God himself. As his servant Thorold confides to Serafina Pekkala: 'his ambition is limitless. He dares to do what men and women don't even dare to think.'

Thorold goes on to say that this makes him either 'mad, wicked, deranged' or else a man like no other, exceeding even angels in his desire and ultimate capacity to put right an ancient wrong. But his pride, so important in motivating him for his great task, also blinds him to the value of others, in particular his own daughter. Only in the closing pages of the trilogy does he realise that her life is actually more important than his own. By this time he has understood that his determination to live in other worlds has been fundamentally mistaken. As the ghost of Will's father John Parry observes: 'we have to build the republic of heaven where we are, because for us there is no elsewhere.'

This is because a dæmon can only live its full life in the world in which it is born. In the same way, Pullman suggests, we too must always make the best of where we are. But Lord Asriel realises, almost too late, that his loyalties must stay with his own universe and in particular with his daughter. A flawed hero, he always runs the risk of turning into just the type of bullying authority he had made it his life's work to destroy. Sacrificing his life to save Lyra is not just a noble act; it is also a final admission that he is ultimately expendable, and to that extent a servant of fate rather than, as he once believed, its potential master.

Mrs Coulter, the mother of his daughter, is an even less attractive character. A faithful servant of the Church, she is party to numbers of its worst acts and joins in enthusiastically herself with the torturing of a young witch. Manipulative, scheming, insincere and ruthless, she is the mother from hell. Flattering Lyra with soft words and shows of affection at one moment, acting like a cruel bully the next, she is never to be trusted. Unlike Lord Asriel, she takes no major role in the great battle between good and evil. Instead she always chooses to play her own game, seeking out every advantage first for herself and then, if it seems convenient, for her employers too.

Mrs Coulter uses her great beauty to maximum effect, charming not just Metatron but also Will, when he is on his mission to rescue Lyra. Sensing his guilt about having been away from his own vulnerable mother for so long, she works on him to the extent that he ends by breaking his precious knife under the emotional strain. But as everyone who temporarily falls for her soon discovers, feminine allure is a false friend unless also accompanied by love and kindness. Like the wicked Queen in *Snow White*, Mrs Coulter is additionally frightening simply because she is so seductively beautiful as well.

Discovering that appearances are often deceptive is a lesson every child has to learn at some stage. Should the person concerned also be their own parent, this lesson can prove a particularly bitter experience. Although most children are more fortunate than Lyra with their mothers, Mrs Coulter's presence in the story is a powerful reminder that evil can be just as bad even when it is hiding behind not just a pretty, but also a familiar face.

So what are readers to make of Mrs Coulter's final discovery that she does love Lyra after all, even to the extent of giving up her own life so that her daughter might live? There is no doubt of her sincerity here, since her author has admitted that it was only when he had got to the end of the trilogy that he discovered for himself that because of her self-sacrifice, Mrs Coulter must indeed have really loved her daughter by this time. But doubts remain whether she genuinely regrets all the other evil things she has done in her life, even though she is fully aware of how low she has descended over the years. Instead, it seems that her maternal instinct, however deeply suppressed before, has at last come to the surface in a way that won't be denied. Having been loved by many other people in vain, she at last has the experience of loving someone back in return. So while Lord Asriel stands for intellectual ambition gone mad, Mrs Coulter symbolises the emotional world of strong, distorted feelings, where self-love battles against an underlying need to provide maternal care when it is most needed.

Both characters also serve as reminders that any final division of characters into good and evil is never easy and often impossible. Just as Milton's Satan has his darkly attractive side, so too do Lord Asriel and Mrs Coulter refuse to behave either entirely admirably or disgracefully. As Pullman has written elsewhere: 'No-one is purely good or purely evil ... I would much rather we thought in terms of good actions, bad actions.'

In his other novels he has also shown that conventionally bad characters can still sometimes get the better of an argument. But despite these qualifications, it is usually clear where Pullman's sympathies lie. This is particularly so with his minor characters, where there is less time to spell out any of their possible accompanying moral complexities. As in the Victorian melodrama and children's adventure comics he so loves, there is no shortage of truly villainous beings in his books, particularly at those moments when it is time for another twist in the plot in order to bring about yet more excitement and suspense.

Influences and Comparisons

John Milton

John Milton's epic poem *Paradise Lost*, written between 1658 and 1663, is one of the greatest literary creations of all time. Drawn from the Old Testament, it sets out to 'justify the ways of God to Men' by retelling the story of how Adam and Eve came to be expelled from the paradise of living in the Garden of Eden. It starts with Satan surrounded by fallen angels who, like him, have been expelled from Heaven to live in the Abyss of Hell. Nothing daunted, he resolves to build the rival kingdom of Pandemonium. But rather than risk another war against God, Satan decides to get back at his hated rival in a more subtle way.

Escaping from Hell, accompanied by his daughter Sin and their joint son Death, Satan sets out to wreck God's plans for His newly created earth. Coming across Adam and Eve living a perfect life untouched by any flaws, guilt or death, Satan starts tempting Eve in dreams to do the only thing she and Adam have been forbidden from doing: eat the fruit from the tree of knowledge. When Adam and Eve refuse, having been warned by the angel Raphael to resist any further temptations on this score, Satan returns disguised as a snake. He tells Eve that God is simply jealous of them and does not want them to become as gods too, which would surely happen once they ate the forbidden apple. Eve finally gives way, and is then joined by Adam, determined now to share her fate. Adam and Eve are expelled from paradise, and in due course, having previously been immortal, must die as the direct result of their one, great sin.

Pullman first came across *Paradise Lost* at the age of sixteen when he studied its first two books at school. Immediately swept away by the majesty of the language and the power of the poetry, he also found it a superb story. In an interview years later he quotes the following lines that he still knows by heart:

> *High on a throne of royal state, which far*
> *Outshone the wealth of Ormus and of Ind,*
> *Or where the gorgeous East with richest hand*
> *Showers on her kings barbaric pearl and gold,*
> *Satan exalted sat, by merit raised*
> *To that bad eminence.*

(Paradise Lost, Book II, lines 1–6)

15. 'High on a throne of royal state, which far / Outshone the wealth of Ormus and of Ind, / Or where the gorgeous East with richest hand / Showers on her kings barbaric pearl and gold, / Satan exalted sat' (II, 1–5). (Source: *Doré's Illustrations for "Paradise Lost"*, Gustave Doré. Copyright © 1993 by Dover Publications, Inc.)

For Pullman, this not only conjures up a vivid and compelling picture; it also raises the questions: 'What's going to happen next? What's he going to do?' So while he went on to reject the theological argument about the Fall of Man on which the poem is based, he was happy to draw much of his inspiration from it. Such borrowings include the phrase *His Dark Materials*, the overall title for his trilogy, which comes from the poem and is quoted just before the first page of *Northern Lights*. It refers to the mixture of water, earth, air and fire involved in the creation of the world and now at large in the wild shores of Hell.

The overlap between *Paradise Lost* and Pullman's trilogy is not exact. While Lord Asriel shares some of Satan's malign energy, he is also an individual in his own right whose life path in the trilogy is never predictable. Nor is Lyra a direct replica of Eve.

In *Paradise Lost*, Milton wrote of Adam and Eve after they have been expelled from paradise:

> *The world was all before them, where to choose*
> *Their place of rest, and Providence their guide;*
> *They hand in hand with wandering steps and slow*
> *Through Eden took their solitary way.*

This is a sad image of two lost souls uncertain where to go next. But in Pullman's reworking of this great poem, Will and Lyra now have the entire world before them as well as their own spirits still intact and ready for the next challenge. The contrast could hardly be greater.

But what the two works do have in common, other than the basic Christian framework from which they make such different deductions, is a richness of imagination. Milton's brooding landscapes are echoed throughout Pullman's work, and there is also a common cast of angels, good and bad. Most importantly, both writers offer readers a trip into an imaginative world where wonders literally never cease but whose central core is still primarily about the eternal struggle between good and evil.

William Blake

Another of Pullman's heroes is the poet and artist William Blake, born in London in 1757. Blake believed that it is in the freedom of the imagination rather than in rational thought that we can best perceive the nature of the divine love and sympathy which surrounds us all. As he wrote in *A Vision of the Last Judgment*: 'If the doors of perception were cleansed everything would appear as it is, infinite.' Only after that can humans hope to discover 'the real and eternal world of which the Vegetable Universe is but a faint shadow'.

Blake was also much taken with the contrast between innocence and experience, writing his most famous sequence of poems around this theme. Several are about a 'Little Girl Lost' whose name is Lyca, a possible inspiration for the Lyra of *His Dark Materials*. The tension between innocence and experience is also a preoccupation with Pullman, who sees advantages in both states, with experience the natural replacement of innocence rather than its inevitable corruption. Blake also believed that the human soul must first pass through the fallen world before it can reach a new, higher state of innocence. This idea is an obvious influence in those scenes in *The Amber Spyglass* where Lyra and Will visit the underworld.

Blake wrote in his principal prose work, *The Marriage of Heaven and Hell*, that the ultimate aim of all humans should be to enter the New Jerusalem of the redeemed imagination. For him, this involves the denial of eternal punishment and ultimate authority – views that have strong connections to Pullman's thinking as well. In *Milton*, one of his last works, Blake portrays the great poet returning from eternity in order to correct his former views about original sin. He now preaches a doctrine of self-sacrifice and forgiveness, and denounces what he has come to see as the evil committed by God.

The principal enemies of the individual when it comes to making the spiritual journey through the fallen world from darkness to light are what Blake described as the various spectres that haunt us and which we must always learn to cast away. For Blake, such spectres are the creation of oppressive religion backed up by the state. His views are summed up in lines from his *Songs of Innocence and Experience*, for example: 'God and his priest and King, who make up a heaven of our misery'. Pullman too describes the equally dangerous and destructive Spectres in his stories as symbolic, in the way that they suck out an individual's soul, causing the type of depression that can render any human life temporarily unbearable.

As part of his denial of the existence of the material world and nothing else, Blake insisted that at times he talked regularly to angels. Pullman also uses angels in his trilogy, along with other mythological or fabulous creatures. This is not because he believes in the everyday existence of such things, but as regularly recurring symbols within the human imagination over the centuries, he clearly thinks that they must by definition stand for something important to all of us. Bringing them into play in a modern story helps build a bridge between today's readers and the most popular fantasies of the past, underlining the continuity of human imagination over the centuries.

Heinrich von Kleist

The third major literary influence upon Pullman, Heinrich von Kleist, was born in 1777 and became an army officer before taking up philosophy. But after reading the works of the great German philosopher Immanuel Kant, Kleist came to the conclusion that human beings would always be incapable of arriving at the absolute truth about anything. Abandoning philosophy in order to become an author, he wrote several plays and many short stories. Eventually sinking into despair, he shot himself in 1811 as part of a suicide pact made with a woman suffering from incurable cancer.

His essay *On the Marionette Theatre* was written a year before his death, and is reprinted in the appendices of this book. Working from the observation that marionettes being set to dance always seem less affected than any human performers, Kleist describes how all individuals, following the example first set by Adam and Eve, have at some stage to become self-conscious. This means that everyone has to lose the child-like spontaneity and grace found in their younger years. The only way to re-enter this former paradise of total lack of self-consciousness is by working through the experience that accompanies adulthood, including those lessons learned through suffering, sorrow and other personal difficulties. So while it may be sad to lose the sort of innocence that marked us out as children, this is no tragedy. Instead, we can use our adult knowledge to recreate the same type of grace again, once we have discovered enough about ourselves and others to acquire the type of wisdom all humans are capable of.

There are obvious connections with *His Dark Materials* here, not least the mention in Kleist's essay of an Iorek-type tethered fighting bear who still manages to get the better of a nobleman armed with a sword and skilled in fencing. Like Kleist, Pullman also sees the story of Adam and Eve as symbolising the way that children have eventually to grow up by eating from the tree of knowledge. But this inevitable step forward should always be seen as an important acquisition rather than as any sort of dreadful loss or crime, because the loss of innocence also marks the beginning of the acquisition of wisdom.

Lyra and Will too have to sacrifice their innocent but sadly impractical desire to spend the rest of their lives together, while Lyra also loses her unconscious ability to work the alethiometer. However, by fully engaging with the life in front of her, she will one day learn how to use the alethiometer again, but this time through hard work rather than through any innate skill. Or as Kleist puts it: 'we must eat again of the tree of knowledge a second time in order to return to the state of innocence'. This particular state is best symbolised by those older characters in *His Dark Materials*, such as Farder Coram, John Faa and Lee Scoresby, whose sound and selfless advice to Lyra is always worth listening to. This is not simply because they have already seen and learned so much during their long lives; it is also because they have reached a level of moral wisdom that only experience linked to self-knowledge can truly bring about.

Pullman, C.S. Lewis and growing up

Although Pullman is on record for despising the Christian-based Narnia stories of C.S. Lewis, the two writers actually share a good deal of background. Both lost a parent when young and later spent most of their adult life in Oxford. Both are fascinated by ideas of 'Northernness', and both create worlds separate from this one where children are put to severe moral tests before finally saving both themselves and everyone else. For both, these tests include withstanding guilt about a sick mother left behind but still in desperate need of a cure. In Lewis's *The Magician's Nephew*, the child Digory is tempted to break a solemn promise by the hope that he might be able to help his sick mother. In *The Subtle Knife*, Will almost gives way when he has a vision of his own mentally ill mother's suffering face just as he is about to wield the knife that will finally cut the world free. Each writer also describes mighty battles within which the good finally manage to defeat the bad.

The Narnia stories famously start with a child making a voyage to another land that exists at the back of a wardrobe. In the opening pages of *Northern Lights*, Lyra too hides inside a wardrobe, shutting the door just as the much-feared steward, who has twice beaten her before, enters the room where she is not supposed to be. This surface similarity between the two stories comes up again at other points. The pitiless Tartars that kidnap Lyra are reminiscent of the Calormenes in

Lewis's *The Last Battle*, with 'their white eyes flashing dreadfully in their brown faces'. Pullman may at other times be deliberately imitating the Narnia stories in order then to highlight the fundamental differences that exist between Lewis's approach and his own.

As Pullman has said himself, he had long 'wanted to give a sort of historical answer to the, so to speak, propaganda on behalf of religion that you get in, for example, C.S. Lewis'. But by attacking Christianity through its own story of the Garden of Eden, Pullman also succeeds in giving at least this part of the Bible an increased visibility that may otherwise have been lost on generations of younger readers. At a time when hearing or reading Bible stories is becoming less common in many schools, some young readers could now find themselves learning about some of the great stories of Christianity from Pullman himself. If this is an irony, Pullman would surely take it in good heart. Brought up on Bible stories as a child, he has never wavered in his love for them purely as stories. It is when they become dogma that he and they part company.

While Lewis follows the orthodox Christian values of his time, Pullman breaks away from them in anger and disgust. In Lewis's *The Last Battle*, one of the main child characters, Susan, is accused by another of the same age of being 'interested in nothing nowadays except nylons and lipstick and invitations. She always was a jolly sight too keen on being grown-up'. Pullman, on the other hand, describes in positive terms the happier times when Lyra learned from her mother how best to apply lipstick, powder and scent. He also welcomes and celebrates the onset of sexuality and the way this changes the relationship between Will and Lyra. In one beautiful passage, Lyra listens to Mary Malone, now taking on the role of serpent in the Garden of Eden. This is because, by talking about an old love affair, she gradually causes Lyra to feel herself coming alive in a new and passionate manner by way of response:

> She felt a stirring at the roots of her hair: she found herself breathing faster. She had never been on a roller-coaster, or anything like one, but if she had, she would have recognized the sensations in her breast: they were exciting and frightening at the same time, and she had not the slightest idea why. The sensation continued, and deepened, and changed, as more parts of her body found themselves affected too.

This lyrical description is reminiscent of the joy felt for each other by Adam and Eve in Book 4 of *Paradise Lost*. They too experienced sexual feelings without any of the attendant guilt that afflicted them later on after they had eaten the apple and then realised, for the first time, that they were both naked and ashamed. But Lyra is presented here as an Eve who is never going to experience the equivalent of the Fall. Will, when he reciprocates her feelings towards him, also feels nothing but tenderness and love. What a pity, Pullman seems to be saying here, that the sexual instinct has not always been celebrated in this way rather than seen through the distorted lens of religiously based disgust.

In Pullman's trilogy, Will and Lyra end their story determined to live their lives in the here and now. They have already discovered that the best way to survive the afterlife is to take with them as many positive stories about their former life as possible, of the type that are enjoyed at the time and then remembered with pleasure and affection afterwards. But the essence of all these stories must be their truthfulness, even if this means sometimes recalling painful as well as pleasurable moments and events from the past.

Even more importantly, they have just fallen in love and exchanged first, passionate embraces. This moment occurs just after Lyra offers Will some of the sweet-tasting red fruit packed for them by Mary Malone that morning. The symbolism is clear: Eve once again is offering fruit to Adam, but now that the Church and Christianity have finally been sent packing there is no one else around to tell them that what feels so good is in fact wicked and bad.

Except, however, for the lone assassin Father Gomez, who for a few moments has Lyra in the telescopic sites of his powerful rifle and is about to pull the trigger. But he is eliminated at the last moment by Balthamos, one of the good angels, just as Eve was once given support by those angels still fighting against the tyranny of Heaven. In the Bible story, Eve lost; in this one, she wins. And at the same moment, 'The Dust pouring down from the stars had found a living home again, and these children-no-longer-children, saturated with love, were the cause of it all'. The victory of the new Adam and Eve is therefore complete. Humanity itself, having previously taken the false path of shame and guilt, can now follow in the same direction as Will and Lyra, unhampered by the past and full of hope for the future.

In the final book of the Narnia series, *The Last Battle*, the children discover that the land they are in is actually heaven. Without realising it, they have all been killed in a railway accident, but find that they are now so happy and fulfilled that they no longer miss any of their former times on earth. But Pullman takes a totally different view in his novels. For him, life on earth is the best there is ever going to be. The contrast could hardly be greater.

There still remains a mountain for Will and Lyra to climb, even so. Pullman has no truck with the idea that childhood is that period of innocence when we are closer to the divine. He has always hated the sort of children's literature that for him 'wallows in a sort of sticky nostalgia for nursery teas, and teddy bear, and bath-time, and wishes it had never grown up'. However happy it might have been: 'We cannot dwell forever in the paradise of childhood, we have to go forward, through the disappointments and compromises and betrayals of experience, towards the fully conscious kind of grace that we call wisdom. Innocence is not wise, and wisdom cannot be innocent.' The compensations of maturity remain huge but they must necessarily be hard won.

The occasional overlaps that do exist between Lewis and Pullman arise for a variety of reasons. Both are authors with a strong sense of mission. Their sense of a world divided between good and evil, and the way that all individuals have to take sides in this eternal battle, actually have a lot in common. Where they differ is over the whole question of Christianity. But at other times, particularly when the forces of light are battling it out with the powers of darkness, they become far more alike. At these moments, neither writer has much time for moral ambiguity in their books. Always happy to fight the good fight, both have little patience with waverers and the fainthearted. Readers who have previously enjoyed the Narnia stories might therefore find much in *His Dark Materials* that could seem pleasantly familiar as well as deeply enjoyable in its own right.

Pullman's Philosophy

In the lecture given on his own concept of the Republic of Heaven, Pullman quotes G.K. Chesterton's remark that once people stop accepting organised religion they will in future believe not so much in nothing but in anything. There are moments in the trilogy when Pullman too seems attracted to alternative belief structures, such as the I Ching form of reading the future originating from China. But at base *His Dark Materials* is a strongly humanist text, celebrating the abiding existence of human courage and essential goodness outside any omnipotent and omniscient supernatural context.

Pullman has said that we can remain true to ourselves and to everyone else by constantly renewing our human faith not by religious belief but with the aid of those stories that remind us of the best we should aspire to. For Pullman: 'They are easily the most important things in the world. Within them we can find the most memorable, life-enhancing glimpses of human beings at their very best.' These are the same types of stories that the ghosts and harpies in *The Amber Spyglass* need in order to renew hope in their place of suffering.

But everyone needs good stories, not just ghosts. In his lecture, quoted above, Pullman writes that: 'A republic that's only believed because it *makes more sense* or it's *more reasonable* than the alternative would be a pallid place indeed, and it wouldn't last for long. What induces that leap of commitment is an emotional thing – a story.' And by writing a best-seller that has given pleasure and consolation to many thousands of readers of all ages and nationalities, Pullman has provided such a story himself.

But if it is human folly and greed that is responsible for what Pullman sees as the crippling religious myths that he attacks in his trilogy, what force or forces produce the ghouls, cliff-ghasts and various other apparitions that appear throughout his story? There is no answer to this question, just as there is no explanation in his books for the existence throughout history of closed, evil minds over and beyond anything that could possibly be attributed to the malign influence of organised Christianity.

It would be mistaken to blame Pullman for this. He is writing a story, not a work of philosophy or history. His own strong views form an important part of what he writes, but it is as a work of fiction that these novels should be assessed. If there are inconsistencies in his judgements or gaps in his arguments, these only matter if belief in the story itself also becomes stretched as a result. To date, there are no signs that this has ever been the case with his multitude of readers, young and old.

Nor is Pullman interested in working out a complete cosmology for the largely imaginary worlds he is describing. Unlike the sagas of J.R.R. Tolkien, there are no accompanying maps in *His Dark Materials*. Nor are there any notes on the language, history and geography of the different people and objects of the type included by Tolkien in *The Lord of the Rings*. Although Pullman shares Tolkien's belief in the huge importance of story in the human imagination, he has no wish to treat his own particular tales as if they were truly describing something real.

Yet as an experienced storyteller, used to entertaining first his own brother as a child and then the various pupils he later taught in schools, Pullman also knows that outsize villains help make good tales. Most of the supernatural nasties in his books simply exist in their own right without any reason or explanation. Readers are unlikely to object, since it is these same evil forces that give the trilogy some of its most memorable moments.

So while the reason for the persistence of evil in human affairs is only partially explained in the trilogy, it does seem clear that dæmons play a large part where individual health and happiness are concerned. When Spectres suck out these dæmons, or when the dæmons themselves have been cut away from their owners, individuals become mere shadows of themselves. They are also open to every enemy that might now come their way unopposed.

Dæmons therefore have much in common with the religious concept of the soul, particularly in those cases where the dæmon is internalised and can't therefore be seen. It is always potentially at risk simply because it is so precious, and must be carefully tended and listened to at all times. Will comes to the conclusion, for example, that his mother's madness was caused by invisible Spectres trying to get a grip on her own dæmon, spirit, soul or whatever other word is used to stand for the moral core of a human being. To lose a soul, or to live with a corrupted one, as Mrs Coulter does with her golden-monkey dæmon, is to live in a spiritual desert. The legendary Dr Faust or the apprentice Karl in Pullman's story *Clockwork*, who both make a pact with the devil involving the selling of their own soul, are as doomed as any of the dæmonless zombies found in Pullman's fiction.

As for the Spectres, old Giacomo Paradisi tells Will and Lyra that they 'are our fault, our fault alone. They came because my predecessors, alchemists, philosophers, men of learning, were making an enquiry into the deepest nature of things. They became curious about the bonds that held the smallest particles of matter together ... We undid them, and we let the Spectres in.' He adds that where the Spectres actually came from remains a mystery, but 'what matters is that they are here, and they have destroyed us'.

This makes Spectres symbolic of what can go wrong when

humankind meddles with matters that should be left alone. An equivalent destructive curiosity found in our own world might arguably include the sort of scientific enquiry that led to the development of nuclear weapons and, later on, to controlled genetic mutations. But there is another possible explanation for Spectres which reaches into the psychological rather than into history or politics. The description of what happens to Lena the witch after a Spectre invades her body is also like reading about a bad attack of depression.

These feelings of ultimate despair also become a possibility every time an individual decides to open a window into a parallel world with the intention of taking up permanent residence there. Pullman may be making a comparison here with those who find themselves spending too long in their own imaginary worlds, suggesting that if they stay away from reality for too long they can eventually risk alienation or even madness. For once the real world comes to seem a poor, uninviting place by comparison, the incentive to return to it may increasingly diminish. Those who want to make the return journey may also discover that the beings in this imaginary world are not always as benign as they might first appear.

The classic description of this process is found in Joanne Greenberg's autobiographical novel, *I Never Promised You a Rose Garden*. The mentally ill narrator, with the help of a sensitive psychotherapist, finally tries to leave the fantasy world she has been content to live in for the real one instead. She then discovers that the imaginary friends who once meant so much to her now turn into pitiless tormentors, anxious to prevent her return to reality – and therefore her cure – at all costs. As a believer in the necessity for living to the full in the world as we know it, Pullman might be hinting here that Spectres do indeed stand for the type of depressive illness that can strike against the very will to live itself. As a metaphor, this is as good as any for describing the process whereby an individual suffering from depression sometimes seems to lose touch altogether with the essential, inner spirit necessary for their personality to function normally.

The best fantasy writing has always meant quite different things to different readers, so there can never be a definitive answer as to what exactly Spectres, or indeed any other characters in Pullman's work, are intended to symbolise. Stories have always had the power to stimulate strong, imaginative reactions in readers, even though these reactions may differ radically from one person to another. The term 'mythopoeic' is used to define writing powerful enough to create its own myths and in doing so give shape to readers' various fears and fantasies. On this basis alone, Pullman's trilogy is an outstanding mythopoeic achievement. In an age in search of new myths to replace some of the older ones from former years, *His Dark Materials* is a text that has already talked directly to thousands. It provides not just entertainment but also extra meaning to many readers and to their own most personal fantasies.

Is there a paradox in the way that Pullman, an anti-Christian, uses Christian symbolism throughout his writing?

Angels both good and bad, Adam and Eve, prophecy and the idea of destiny, images of pilgrimage, the importance of the soul and the notion of heaven and hell all play vital parts in his narrative. Milton and Blake, both widely quoted, were Christian writers, and there are also quotations from the Bible and Christian poets such as George Herbert and Andrew Marvell.

But although the architecture and symbolism in *His Dark Materials* largely derive from Christian sources, the emphasis is mostly on how it all went wrong. In this sense, the trilogy is not so much an atheist text as a reworking of a Christian one towards radically different conclusions. As an intensely moral writer, Pullman seems naturally drawn towards Biblical imagery of good and evil of the type that has played such a key part in the history of the Western world. Yet he is also aware of other ways to spiritual truth found in different cultures, and there are references in *His Dark Materials* to Buddhism, Pantheism, Paganism and I Ching as alternative ways towards ultimate understanding.

He also refers to Gnosticism, condemned early on as a heresy by the Church, which has as its basic tenet the belief that knowledge of transcendence can only be experienced personally and intuitively. Humans in this view are of the same essence as God but as long as our spirits are trapped in physical bodies there will always be sin. Salvation, therefore, is to escape from the bondage of material existence and travel back to the home from which our souls have originally fallen.

God meanwhile is far removed from the world which was in fact created by an evil, lesser God, sometimes called a demi-urge. Pullman has written that this system of belief 'seems to speak very directly' to our psychological and spiritual condition, although he dislikes its denigration of the physical universe. But his main point here, as elsewhere, is always the same: different systems of belief may well suit different people. The mistake, and indeed crime, is to insist upon just one as the only permitted way for any individual to seek out their own personal truth.

As a humanist and freethinker himself, he hates the guilt and repression that, in his view, also lie at the basis of Christianity, particularly how it was practised in the past. The end result is a story that sets out not so much to demolish the value of the religious impulse experienced by so many human beings but to push it in a totally different direction. Believing that there is more to life than simple materialism, he creates instead an alternative vision of the world that shares a Christian notion of a divine presence somewhere and somehow, but rejects all the definitions and claimed manifestations of it of the type recorded in the Bible.

Fundamentalist Christians reject the theory of evolution, preferring to believe that God himself created all known species. Evolutionists take an opposite line, convinced that Darwin's theory of natural selection shows how species can change without any need of divine intervention. Pullman too belongs to this particular camp, but adds that now humans are on the scene there is also the chance to direct future development rather than simply wait passively for more evolutionary change.

All the living beings on earth found in *His Dark Materials* are the result of evolution. One example of this is demonstrated to Mary Malone when she learns about the ways that the mulefa have developed over the centuries through constant interaction with the seed-pods that are so important to them. Pullman himself has described the process of human evolution as blind and automatic, and accepts the Darwinian notion of natural selection as the only acceptable explanation for how it all works. But because humans have consciousness, he also believes that this potentially alters the future processes of evolution. As he says in his lecture on the Republic of Heaven: 'We might have arrived by a series of accidents, but from now on we have to take charge of our fate. Now we are here, now we are conscious, we make a difference. Our presence changes everything.'

In *His Dark Materials*, Will and Lyra show how two people can have a profound effect upon the future as well as the present. But their victory is hard won rather than inevitable, and if some of the evil characters had prevailed instead, the outcome would have been disastrous. So although Pullman believes that human beings can make all the difference in the way that their own species continues to adapt to the world, he also makes it clear that such change always has the potential to be either good or bad.

Developments
Since Publication of
His Dark Materials

Much has been written and argued over about
Pullman's trilogy since it was first published. The
release of the filmed version of the first instalment,
The Golden Compass, in 2007 led to denunciations from
some American Roman Catholic and evangelical sources
along with a plea for a general boycott. This was despite a
general playing down in the film of Pullman's original questioning of religion. With only moderate box office returns,
particularly in America, plans for a further two films were
abandoned. Critical reaction was mixed. It was generally
agreed that Nicole Kidman made a compelling Mrs Coulter
and Daniel Craig a suitably Byronic Lord Asriel. Visual effects
were also held to be excellent, winning their own Oscar. But
despite scene cuts and some altered chronology, character

development remained insufficient in an increasingly confused story where too much happened too quickly, until the arrival of a final battle sequence that this time lasted too long.

There was little corresponding Christian backlash in Britain, either about the film or the trilogy. This may be because Pullman himself was never any sort of militant atheist. Instead, as he said at the time in an interview: 'I've got no evidence whatever for believing in a God. But I know that all the things I do know are very small compared with the things that I don't know. So maybe there is a God out there.' Still believing that Bible stories are an essential part of children's education, he came over more as an agnostic with an instinctively religious outlook.

As Hugh Rayment-Pickard puts it in his book, *The Devil's Account: Philip Pullman and Christianity*: Pullman offers a humanistic religion of life and love in place of the Christian myth of fall and redemption.'

Other radical theologians, meanwhile, share a position not far from Pullman's. In his book *Original Blessing: a Primer in Creation Spirituality*, published in 1983, Matthew Fox argues that the essential good of creation should always have been seen as far more significant than any accompanying idea of original sin. Original sin replaced by the notion of original blessing is utterly in sympathy with Pullman's own system of beliefs.

In two well-tempered debates held between Pullman and the then Archbishop of Canterbury Rowan Williams in 2004, both sides were often in close agreement, particularly when discussing the vital importance of mythology in the human imagination. For Pullman, in one such discussion, mythology is something 'whose truth is not historical truth only but has a truth that also sort of lives on'. Hence his passionate belief in the power of story, however hard this may be to define or even articulate. Elsewhere, he has frequently been quoted in his support for the poet John Keats, who in a letter to a friend wrote about the virtues of what he termed negative capability, defined in his own words as the state of mind when 'man is capable of being in uncertainties, Mysteries, doubts, without any irritable reaching after fact and reason'. Those who try and have tried questioning Pullman over the years on the exact meanings of passages in *His Dark Materials* should not be surprised when he falls back on a similar defence of ultimate uncertainty rather than coming up with any over-specific answers.

In 2010 Pullman's novel of ideas, *The Good Man Jesus and the Scoundrel Christ*, was published. Its title proved more provocative than its text. Jesus here remains the preacher and miracle-worker of the New Testament who was eventually crucified. But towards the end of his life he loses faith in God. He also starts dreading what might happen should his own beliefs become part of an established religion, open to abuse from those intent on controlling it in order to further their own power. But after his death this is exactly what happens, with his twin brother Christ posing as Jesus and developing a doctrine that his dead brother never taught, while deceiving others with lies about his Resurrection. Pullman suggests, by the end, that we should return to what the original Jesus said while rejecting church doctrines that both spread and subsequently distorted his essential gospel message. Some of Pullman's Christian critics since have found this notion not unsympathetic.

In 2012 Pullman brought out his version of *Grimm Tales*: favourite stories collected by the brothers Grimm. He claims in his introduction only to be interested in getting these tales across in the best way he can as working and effective stories for all time. Much as he has always loved them he has elsewhere denied the existence of any obvious fairy tale influence on *His Dark Materials*. The qualities he finds in these stories, such as pace rather than characterisation, and arbitrary happenings rather than psychological realism, are indeed not associated with his own writing. But Pullman loves them for the special quality that has enabled them to last for so long. What this final quality is never becomes clear and may well be, in his own words, something that is 'too easy for children and too difficult for adults'. This is another reminder that for Pullman, stories need only justify themselves by their own excellence as fiction, leaving each reader to draw from them the memories, lessons, hopes and fears that exist most urgently in their own imagination.

Critical reaction to *His Dark Materials* over the years has proved largely positive. Some critics writing from a

Christian perspective continue to take issue with what they see as Pullman's attack upon the worst aspects of the history of their religion without taking into account any of its positive attributes. They have also pointed out that atheistic political regimes today can be quite as cruel as any of their Christian counterparts in the past. Feminist critics, on the other hand, have sometimes objected to the way that Will starts to dominate Lyra, particularly in *The Amber Spyglass*, when it comes to generally taking the lead. Others have complained about what they see as traces of social snobbery in the narrative, with Lyra, very much a child of destiny, the daughter of exceptional and glamorous parents. Humbler persons, by contrast, are often given away by the nature of their dæmons, with servants' dæmons almost invariably pictured as dogs, or other domesticated animals. There have also been objections to the way that dæmons remain fixed and immutable once adulthood has been reached. Does this suggest that adults are incapable of further growth and change for the rest of their lives?

But on the whole Pullman's achievements, celebrated when the trilogy first came out, have continued to attract far more praise than blame. In an article for *The New Yorker*, Laura Miller has written that: '*His Dark Materials* may be the first fantasy series founded upon the ideals of the Enlightenment rather than upon tribal and mythic yearnings for kings, gods and supermen.' It seemed highly appropriate, therefore that in 2008 Pullman received an International

Humanist Award from the World Humanist Congress. But for Hugh Rayment-Picard, in *His Dark Materials*, so often rooted in the texts about which it is so critical, Pullman 'tries to out-narrate Christianity [...] with a myth that is simply more appealing more powerful, and more convincing than the Christian narrative.' As Pullman himself has always insisted, tell a good story and people will always find their own meanings in it. And there has never been any question that *His Dark Materials* amounts to three very good stories indeed.

Conclusion

At the moment when Will and Lyra shyly handle each other's dæmons for the first time, they cease to be children. From this time forward, their dæmons will take on a permanent shape, and Will and Lyra will move towards that adult state which, throughout the trilogy, is always shown as naturally attracting more Dust than was the case with childhood. Dust, mislabelled by Christianity and the Church as original sin, clearly stands in this context for a state of heightened self-consciousness, linked in this case to a first experience of sexual delight. How far Lyra and Will actually go down this road is deliberately left unclear, with Pullman himself admitting that: 'They have their moment of bliss – whatever it is (and I don't know what it is).' But given their tender ages, any first expression of physical love – even a passionate embrace – has the capacity to come over as an event of such mind-blowing proportions that ordinary life may indeed never seem the same afterwards.

The end of childish innocence that accompanies first sexual consciousness is also associated with the beginning of adult wisdom. So although Lyra can no longer read her alethiometer, having lost the particular state of innocent grace that once enabled her to do so, she can still recover this skill through hard work. As the angel Xaphania puts it to her: 'Your reading will be even better then, after a lifetime of thought and effort, because it will come from conscious understanding. Grace attained like that is deeper and fuller than grace that comes freely, and furthermore, once you've gained it, it will never leave you.'

This, then, is the journey that the first Eve also had to take after she ate the apple that symbolised sexual and intellectual awareness. Lyra has to make it too, but now she is unpunished by those ecclesiastical forces that vilified the first Eve and have done their level best to eliminate the second one. She can therefore come into her adulthood without shame, showing her fellow humans an altogether better way to live and in so doing destroying the negative powers of the Church for ever. This she achieves when her own new-found state of happiness and fulfilment goes on to fill the rest of the world with the same vivid sense of loving awareness, while she and Will 'lay together as the earth turned slowly and the moon and stars blazed above them'.

By leading the suffering ghosts from the underworld of the dead, Lyra also puts right one last great wrong that occurred when Adam and Eve were expelled from the Garden of Eden. Previously immortal, they were then told of the certainty one day of their own death. But liberating the ghosts, by allowing them back into a world where they can now happily disappear, replaces the Christian notion of death with the idea of a natural re-absorption into the atmosphere. Any idea of eternal punishment in hell or reward in heaven is therefore dropped in favour once again of another type of immortality. For although all ghosts disappear once they leave the underworld, they will still always be present in an invisible world where they are now at peace with everything else. Lord Asriel's original prophecy in *Northern Lights*, that death itself was going to die, therefore finally comes about, although he had not known at the time that it was his daughter who was going to deliver this essential freedom rather than himself.

By making Will and Lyra – like Romeo and Juliet – separate just as they have finally found each other, Pullman also ensures that this first vision of young love remains forever unsullied by any of the practical difficulties or inevitable disagreements that creep into even the most ideal of human relationships. It would, in fact, have been difficult to imagine these two characters from different worlds living happily together in either one or the other place for the rest of their lives. Both have a lot of growing up to do, with neither of their worlds looking particularly kindly upon a passionate love affair between two people so young. But as the last and most powerful symbol in the trilogy, love at its first and most intense still serves Pullman's overall message well. It makes an unforgettable case for the way that humans can, and should, always seek to discover and realise the state of heaven that lies within and between themselves rather than forever looking for it elsewhere.

Even so, some have found this final separation something of an anti-climax. Will and Lyra resolving to spend the rest of their lives properly and constructively in their separate worlds is admirable in itself, but hardly measures up against the enormity of their loss. When the angel Xaphania tells them how to set about living a good life, she sounds more like an old-fashioned schoolmistress than a divine presence. As she puts it, Lyra and Will can preserve the precious Dust now flowing back into the world by helping others 'to learn and understand about themselves and each other and the way everything works, and by showing them how to be kind instead of cruel, and patient instead of hasty, and cheerful instead of surly, and above all how to keep their minds open and free and curious.'

It is also implicit in Pullman's writing that Will and Lyra have it within them to overcome their loss by determining to give their all to the life they have remaining to them. Only then will they be able to play their part in building the Republic of Heaven which, to a certain extent, must always rely upon those concerned giving up some of what they most want in order to benefit everyone else. Had either Will or Lyra insisted on the other going with them to their world, this act of putting their own needs first would have made it impossible for them then to live the sort of life they were hoping for. It would also have deprived readers of an ending that remains extremely moving because it is also so sad.

So the whole idea of going off with each other, rather than staying in their old worlds, represents a final temptation for Will and Lyra to put their own good above everything else. The first Eve fell for the temptation of acquiring true knowledge and understanding, and again Pullman thinks she was right to do so. Lyra, the second Eve, resists the temptation

16. The botanic gardens, Oxford. At the end of *The Amber Spyglass*, Will and Lyra agree to go to the same bench in these gardens in their separate worlds – at midday on Midsummer's Day every year for as long as they live.

of selfishness, and this time Pullman is on her side. For a true Republic of Heaven needs people who 'have to be all those difficult things like cheerful and kind and curious and brave and patient, and we've got to study and think, and work hard, all of us, in all our different worlds'. Backing up this fairly demanding summons, Pullman quotes the great nineteenth-century writer George Eliot's comment after talking about God, Immortality and Duty: 'How inconceivable the first, how unbelievable the second and yet how peremptory and absolute the third.'

Pullman adds himself: 'I like this earnestness. I admire it a great deal.' Yet he feels something to be lacking here, which for him is the accompanying sense of joy that he also believes is a natural, as well as necessary, part of living. Even so, it is perhaps ironic that a trilogy written against Christianity should end on this note of self-denial. The angel's message urging Lyra and Will towards making an even greater effort in their future lives would not have been out of place in those many improving children's books from the past that regularly used to carry a Christian message as well.

Pullman is a strongly idealistic writer, naturally drawn to other thinkers and authors who have also striven to find morals and meanings in the universe. At a time when Christianity was the universal belief, it is inevitable that these voices were mostly Christian at base, whatever their occasional surface disagreements with organised religion. But in a modern Western world where the orthodox Christian story looks to many increasingly remote and unbelievable, Pullman provides readers with a different type of spiritual journey.

His Dark Materials is written in a religious framework in the sense that it also searches for an ultimate meaning to the age-old problem facing all readers of why exactly they are here and what they should then be doing about it. Yet while Christianity sought answers to this question in the theology Pullman so dislikes, he meets this challenge through the imagination. For it is in stories, and the way they can renew faith both in ourselves and in others, that he has always chosen to operate, and never more effectively than in this particular trilogy. Its large sales suggest that in an increasingly Godless age the appetite still remains for literature that powerfully engages readers with its own type of spiritual quest.

Uniquely for a book written for children, *The Amber Spyglass* won the Whitbread Award in 2001 for the best book of the year. It was also long-listed for the Booker Prize – another award normally going to novels written with only an adult audience in mind. Having once produced school plays that entertained both parents and pupils, Pullman has now achieved the same aim with these books. This success was particularly gratifying for him, given that he has always believed that the best children's literature has universal appeal. As he said in his acceptance speech when winning the Carnegie Medal in 1995 for *Northern Lights*: 'Only in children's literature is the story taken seriously.'

In the same vein, he has stated elsewhere that: 'Children's books still deal with the huge themes which have always been part of literature – love, loyalty, the place of religion and science in life, what it really means to be human. Contemporary adult fiction is too small and sterile for what I'm trying to do.' The great success of his trilogy suggests that the desire among all ages for novels which take up these big themes is as strong as ever.

There is also a universal need for convincing fantasy where the good finally prosper and the bad come to a sorry end. In real life it is often hard to tell which the good side is and even harder to assess whether it truly does come off better at the finish. A story that raises such questions and then comprehensively answers them clearly has a lot going for it. But no book ever survives on the merits of its ideas alone. *His Dark Materials* is also written in language that is clear, direct and easy on the ear. There is no tired English in this saga. The windy rhetoric found in some other fantasy sagas is avoided in favour of short sentences that say exactly what they mean, even when there is something complex to get across.

Pullman has himself spoken about how best to write in a lecture delivered in New York in April 2002:

> The aim must always be clarity. It's tempting to feel that if a passage of writing is obscure, it must be very deep. But if the water is murky, the bottom might be only an inch below the surface – you just can't tell. It's much

better to write in such a way that the readers can see all the way down; but that's not the end of it, because you then have to provide interesting things down there for them to look at. Telling a story involves thinking of some interesting events, putting them in the best order to bring out the connections between them, and telling about them as clearly as we can.

To read these books aloud, as Pullman has done as the narrator in an audio version, is to experience at first hand how easily they flow and how well each character is caught. If the many younger readers who have enjoyed these books also pick up some of Pullman's limpid prose style at the same time, they will be learning from someone who is a master not just of the imagination but also of written English. Equally at home with both everyday dialogue and with those moments when his imagination soars to meet the challenge of describing scenes of great, sometimes unearthly, beauty, he has never written better or to greater effect. His trilogy, with its extraordinary power and unforgettable impact, represents the culmination of a long apprenticeship in writing, starting off the day after he left university and finally climaxing in one of the most ambitious and far-reaching works of imagination ever to appear in either children's or adult fiction.

BIBLIOGRAPHY

Books by Philip Pullman

Galatea, London: Gollancz, 1978; New York: Dutton, 1979

Count Karlstein, or the Ride of the Demon Huntsman, London: Chatto and Windus, 1982

Count Karlstein, or the Ride of the Demon Huntsman, graphic-novel version illustrated by Patrice Aggs, London: Doubleday, 1991

Count Karlstein, or the Ride of the Demon Huntsman, with a new introduction, London: Doubleday, 2002

The Ruby in the Smoke, Oxford: Oxford University Press, 1985

How To Be Cool, London: Heinemann, 1987

The Shadow in the North, Oxford: Oxford University Press, 1987

Spring-Heeled Jack; a Story of Bravery and Evil, London: Transworld, 1989

The Broken Bridge, London: Macmillan, 1990

The Tiger in the Well, Harmondsworth: Penguin, 1992

The White Mercedes (The Butterfly Tattoo), London: Macmillan, 1992

The Tin Princess, London: Penguin, 1994

Thunderbolt's Waxwork, London: Viking, 1994

The Firework-Maker's Daughter, London: Doubleday, 1995

The Gas-Fitters' Ball, London: Penguin, 1995

Northern Lights (His Dark Materials: Book One), London: Scholastic, 1995. Published with the title *The Golden Compass* in the USA, New York: Knopf, 1996

Clockwork, or All Wound Up, London: Doubleday, 1996

The Subtle Knife (His Dark Materials: Book Two), London: Scholastic, 1997

Mossycoat, London: Scholastic, 1998

I Was a Rat, or The Scarlet Slippers, London: Doubleday, 1999

The Amber Spyglass (His Dark Materials: Book Three), London: Scholastic, 2000

Puss in Boots, London: Doubleday, 2000

The Scarecrow and His Servant, London: Doubleday, 2004

The Good Man Jesus and the Scoundrel Christ, Edinburgh: Canongate, 2010

Grimm Tales for Young and Old, London: Penguin, 2012

Plays by Philip Pullman

Frankenstein, adaptation of the novel by Mary Shelley,
 Oxford: Oxford University Press, 1990

*Sherlock Holmes and the Adventure of the Limehouse
 Horror*, London: Nelson, 1992

Secondary Sources

Butler, Catherine and Halsdorf, Tommy (eds), *Philip
 Pullman: His Dark Materials* London: Macmillan, 2014

Colbert, David, *The Magical Worlds of Philip Pullman*,
 London: Penguin, 2006

Gribbin, John and Mary, *The Science of Philip Pullman's* His
 Dark Materials, London: Hodder, 2003

Lenz, Millicent and Scott, Carole (eds), *His Dark Materials
 Illuminated*, Detroit: Wayne State University Press,
 2005

Pullman, P., *One Way Home*, part of a series of
 conversations with authors and psychoanalysts,
 London: Institute of Psychoanalysis, 2003

Rayment-Picard, Hugh, *The Devil's Account: Philip Pullman
 and Christianity*, London: Darton, Longman and Todd,
 2004

Simpson, Paul, *The Rough Guide to Philip Pullman's* His
 Dark Materials, London: Rough Guides, 2007

Squires, Claire, *Philip Pullman – Master Storyteller: A
 Guide to the World of* His Dark Materials, London:
 Continuum, 2007

Appendix

On the Marionette Theatre

by Heinrich von Kleist
Translated by Idris Parry

One evening in the winter of 1801 I met an old friend in a public park. He had recently been appointed principal dancer at the local theatre and was enjoying immense popularity with the audiences. I told him I had been surprised to see him more than once at the marionette theatre which had been put up in the market-place to entertain the public with dramatic burlesques interspersed with song and dance. He assured me that the mute gestures of these puppets gave him much satisfaction and told me bluntly that any dancer who wished to perfect his art could learn a lot from them.

From the way he said this I could see it wasn't something which had just come into his mind, so I sat down to question him more closely about his reasons for this remarkable assertion.

He asked me if I hadn't in fact found some of the dance movements of the puppets (and particularly of the smaller ones) very graceful. This I couldn't deny. A group of four peasants dancing the rondo in quick time couldn't have been painted more delicately by Teniers.

I inquired about the mechanism of these figures. I wanted to know how it is possible, without having a maze of strings attached to one's fingers, to move the separate limbs and extremities in the rhythm of the dance. His answer was that I must not imagine each limb as being individually positioned and moved by the operator in the various phases of the dance. Each movement, he told me, has its centre of gravity; it is enough to control this within the puppet. The limbs, which are only pendulums, then follow mechanically of their own accord, without further help. He added that this movement is very simple. When the centre of gravity is moved in a straight line, the limbs describe curves. Often shaken in a purely haphazard way, the puppet falls into a kind of rhythmic movement which resembles dance.

This observation seemed to me to throw some light at last on the enjoyment he said he got from the marionette theatre, but I was far from guessing the inferences he would draw from it later.

I asked him if he thought the operator who controls these puppets should himself be a dancer or at least have some idea of beauty in the dance. He replied that if a job is technically easy it doesn't follow that it can be done entirely without sensitivity. The line the centre of gravity has to follow is indeed very simple, and in most cases, he believed, straight. When it is curved, the law of its curvature seems to be at the least of the first and at the most of the second order. Even in the latter case the line is only elliptical, a form of movement natural to the human body because of the joints, so this hardly demands any great skill from the operator. But, seen from another point of view, this line could be something very mysterious. It is nothing other than *the path taken by the soul of the dancer.* He doubted if this could be found unless the operator can transpose himself into the centre of gravity of the marionette. In other words, the operator *dances*.

I said the operator's part in the business had been represented to me as something which can be done entirely without feeling – rather like turning the handle of a barrel-organ.

'Not at all', he said. 'In fact, there's a subtle relationship between the movements of his fingers and the movements of the puppets attached to them, something like the relationship between numbers and their logarithms or between asymptote and hyperbola.' Yet he did believe this last trace of human volition could be removed from the marionettes and their dance transferred entirely to the realm of mechanical forces, even produced, as I had suggested, by turning a handle.

I told him I was astonished at the attention he was paying to this vulgar species of an art form. It wasn't just that he thought it capable of loftier development; he seemed to be working to this end himself.

He smiled. He said he was confident that, if he could get a craftsman to construct a marionette to the specifications he had in mind, he could perform a dance with it which neither he nor any other skilled dancer of his time, not even Madame Vestris herself, could equal.

'Have you heard,' he asked, as I looked down in silence, 'of those artificial legs made by English craftsmen for people who have been unfortunate enough to lose their own limbs?' I said I hadn't. I had never seen anything of this kind.

'I'm sorry to hear that,' he said, 'because when I tell you these people dance with them, I'm almost afraid you won't believe me. What am I saying ... dance? The range of their movements is in fact limited, but those they can perform they execute with a certainty and ease and grace which must astound the thoughtful observer.'

I said with a laugh that of course he had now found his man. The craftsman who could make such remarkable limbs could surely build a complete marionette for him, to his specifications.

'And what,' I asked, as he was looking down in some perplexity, 'are the requirements you think of presenting to the ingenuity of this man?'

'Nothing that isn't to be found in these puppets we see here,' he replied: 'proportion, flexibility, lightness ... but all to a higher degree. And especially a more natural arrangement of the centres of gravity.'

'And what is the advantage your puppets would have over living dancers?'

'The advantage? First of all a negative one, my friend: it would never be guilty of affectation. For affectation is seen, as you know, when the soul, or moving force, appears at some point other than the centre of gravity of the movement. Because the operator controls with his wire or thread only this centre, the attached limbs are just what they should be ... lifeless, pure pendulums, governed only by the law of gravity. This is an excellent quality. You'll look for it in vain in most of our dancers.'

'Just look at that girl who dances Daphne', he went on. 'Pursued by Apollo, she turns to look at him. At this moment her soul seems to be in the small of her back. As she bends she looks as if she's going to break, like a naiad after the school of Bernini. Or take that young fellow who dances Paris when he's standing among the three goddesses and offering the apple to Venus. His soul is in fact located (and it's a frightful thing to see) in his elbow.'

'Misconceptions like this are unavoidable,' he said, 'now that we've eaten of the tree of knowledge. But Paradise is locked and bolted, and the cherubim stands behind us. We have to go on and make the journey round the world to see if it is perhaps open somewhere at the back.'

This made me laugh. Certainly, I thought, the human spirit can't be in error when it is non-existent. I could see he had more to say, so I begged him to go on.

'In addition,' he said, 'these puppets have the advantage of being for all practical purposes weightless. They are not afflicted with the inertia of matter, the property most resistant to dance. The force which raises them into the air is greater than the one which draws them to the ground. What would our good Miss G. give to be sixty pounds lighter or to have a weight of this size as a counterbalance when she is performing her entrechats and pirouettes? Puppets need the ground only to glance against lightly, like elves, and through this momentary check to renew the swing of their limbs. We humans must have it to rest on, to recover from the effort of the dance. This moment of rest is clearly no part of the dance. The best we can do is make it as inconspicuous as possible.'

My reply was that, no matter how cleverly he might present his paradoxes, he would never make me believe a mechanical puppet can be more graceful than a living human body. He countered this by saying that, where grace is concerned, it is impossible for man to come anywhere near a puppet. Only a god can equal inanimate matter in this respect. This is the point where the two ends of the circular world meet.

I was absolutely astonished. I didn't know what to say to such extraordinary assertions.

It seemed, he said as he took a pinch of snuff, that I hadn't read the third chapter of the book of Genesis with sufficient attention. If a man wasn't familiar with that initial period of all human development, it would be difficult to have a fruitful discussion with him about later developments and even more difficult to talk about the ultimate situation.

I told him I was well aware how consciousness can disturb natural grace. A young acquaintance of mine had as it were lost his innocence before my very eyes, and all because of a chance remark. He had never found his way back to that Paradise of innocence, in spite of all conceivable efforts. 'But what inferences,' I added, 'can you draw from that?'

He asked me what incident I had in mind.

'About three years ago,' I said, 'I was at the baths with a young man who was then remarkably graceful. He was about fifteen, and only faintly could one see the first traces of vanity, a product of the favours shown him by women. It happened that we had recently seen in Paris the figure of the boy pulling a thorn out of his foot. The cast of the statue is well known; you see it in most German collections. My friend looked into a tall mirror just as he was lifting his foot to a stool to dry it, and he was reminded of the statue. He smiled and told me of his discovery. As a matter of fact, I'd noticed it too, at the same moment, but ... I don't know if it was to test the quality of his apparent grace or to provide a salutary counter to his vanity ... I laughed and said he must be imagining things. He blushed. He lifted his foot a second time, to show me, but the effort was a failure, as anybody could have foreseen. He tried it again a third time, a fourth time, he must have lifted his foot ten times, but it was in vain. He was quite unable to reproduce the same movement. What am I saying? The movements he made were so comical that I was hard put to it not to laugh.

'From that day, from that very moment, an extraordinary change came over this boy. He began to spend whole days before the mirror. His attractions slipped away from him, one after the other. An invisible and incomprehensible power seemed to settle like a steel net over the free play of his gestures. A year later nothing remained of the lovely grace which had given pleasure to all who looked at him. I can tell you of a man, still alive, who was a witness to this strange and unfortunate event. He can confirm it, word for word, just as I've described it.'

'In this connection,' said my friend warmly, 'I must tell you another story. You'll easily see how it fits in here. When I was on my way to Russia I spent some time on the estate of a Baltic nobleman whose sons had a passion for fencing. The elder in particular, who had just come down from the university, thought he was a bit of an expert. One morning, when I was in his room, he offered me a rapier. I accepted his challenge but, as it turned out, I had the better of him. It made him angry, and this increased his confusion. Nearly every thrust I made found its mark. At last his rapier flew into the corner of the room. As he picked it up he said, half in anger and half in jest, that he had met his master but that there is a master for everyone and everything – and now he proposed to lead me to mine. The brothers laughed loudly at this and shouted: 'Come on, down to the shed!' They took me by the hand and led me outside to make the acquaintance of a bear which their father was rearing on the farm.

'I was astounded to see the bear standing upright on his hind legs, his back against the post to which he was chained, his right paw raised ready for battle. He looked me straight in the eye. This was his fighting posture. I wasn't sure if I was dreaming, seeing such an opponent. They urged me to attack. "See if you can hit him!" they shouted. As I had now recovered somewhat from my astonishment I fell on him with my rapier. The bear made a slight movement with his paw and parried my thrust. I feinted, to deceive him. The bear did not move. I attacked again, this time with all the skill I could muster. I know I would certainly have thrust my way through to a human breast, but the bear made a slight movement with his paw and parried my thrust. By now I was almost in the same state as the elder brother had been: the bear's utter seriousness robbed me of my composure. Thrusts and feints followed thick and fast, the sweat poured off me, but in vain. It wasn't merely that he parried my thrusts like the finest fencer in the world; when I feinted to deceive him he made no move at all. No human fencer could equal his perception in this respect. He stood upright, his paw raised ready for battle, his eye fixed on mine as if he could read my soul there, and when my thrusts were not meant seriously he did not move. Do you believe this story?'

'Absolutely,' I said with joyful approval. 'I'd believe it from a stranger, it's so probable. Why shouldn't I believe it from you?'

'Now, my excellent friend,' said my companion, 'you are in possession of all you need to follow my argument. We see that in the organic world, as thought grows dimmer and weaker, grace emerges more brilliantly and decisively. But just as a section drawn through two lines suddenly reappears on the other side after passing through infinity, or as the image in a concave mirror turns up again right in front of us after dwindling into the distance, so grace itself returns when knowledge has as it were gone through an infinity. Grace appears most purely in that human form which either has no consciousness or an infinite consciousness. That is, in the puppet or in the god.'

'Does that mean,' I said in some bewilderment, 'we must eat again of the tree of knowledge in order to return to the state of innocence?'

'Of course,' he said, 'but that's the final chapter in the history of the world.'

1810

Lyra's Oxford

This short story allows readers one more glimpse of Lyra, two years further on and, to her teachers and fellow pupils, now a law-abiding and hard-working schoolgirl. She has changed in other ways too, with her cheerfully ungrammatical spoken English now a thing of the past. Since parting from Will, 'the slightest thing had the power to move her to pity and distress'. No longer the tough heroine of former times, she continuously feels 'as if her heart were bruised for ever'.

This ready sympathy leads her into danger when she is persuaded by a witch's dæmon to follow him into the back streets of Oxford on an apparent errand of mercy. When she and her faithful Pan arrive at their chosen destination, she is nearly murdered. She then meets the mysterious Mr Makepeace, described by others as an alchemist but in fact someone working on a vitally important personal mission. Although he refuses to tell Lyra what this is, he does say that she may find out more in time. It looks as if the ground is being set here for further books in the future. Or as Pullman puts in in his preface: 'This book contains a story and several other things. The other things might be connected with the story, or they might not; they might be connected to stories that haven't appeared yet. It's hard to tell.'

Designed to look like a bundle of documents that could have come from another world, like our own in some ways but different in others, *Lyra's Oxford* also includes some spoof advertisements and postcards as well as a pull-out map of the city. On it, some pretend handwriting in brown ink shows where Mary Malone lives and points the way to the avenue of hornbeam trees where Will first spotted the near-invisible window through which he could pass into Lyra's Oxford. Depictions on the map of steam trains and a Zeppelin station remind readers and the odd unaware tourist that this is not the real Oxford, however similar some of the buildings and the general topography.

But, as always with Pullman, there is a serious point beyond his love of pastiche. Lyra insists twice in this story that everything always means something, and it is up to everyone to find personal significance in the day-to-day details of their ordinary existence. In this story, for example, Lyra and Pan conclude after the event that they were saved by the flocks of birds that attacked the witch's dæmon. While the birds were trying to warn them of impending danger, the city itself also seemed to be giving them its protection. Or at least that is what it felt like, and, as Pullman makes clear, our feelings about things always become part of the meaning we attach to them.

Yet, if everything does indeed mean something, it can still be very difficult to work out exactly what this might be at the time. It is easier instead to look back to the past to understand how exactly what then took place might influence the present. But what if the workings of the universe were so organised that our own futures might also be influencing the choices we make in our daily lives? How could any human expect to be let in to this particular secret? Perhaps Mr Makepeace and his attempts to discover the key to the whole cosmos will one day come up with an answer.

In his preface to *Lyra's Oxford*, we have already seen Pullman writing how it is never easy to tell what may or may not turn out to be important in the course of any particular story. All he can do is narrate the plot as it appears to him at the moment; other meanings, perhaps presently obscured, may become clearer with the passage of time. As in fiction, so also in life. Readers too, by implication, may never be entirely sure about what exactly is happening to them in their daily existence and why. Like novelists, they too must search for their own key to understanding as much as they can, always remembering that what may sometimes look unimportant now could turn out to be far more significant in the long run.

Once Upon a Time in the North

This novella and prequel, set some time before Lyra's birth, features Pullman's favourite character Lee Scoresby, aged 24 and flying the balloon he has recently won in a poker game. A difficult landing finds him in the imaginary harbour town of Novy Odense, set on an island in the Muscovy White Sea. Wandering into town Lee soon becomes aware of the hatred directed at a group of dispirited working bears, despised by some as 'worthless vagrants'. There is also an unmistakable whiff of corruption surrounding a populist mayor seeking re-election and in the pay of Larsen Manganese, a ruthless and dishonest mining company.

Things come to a head when Lee enables a Dutch skipper to rescue his illegally embargoed cargo. Lee is also by this time up against some local ruffians led by his old enemy and hired gun-man Pierre Morton, who had tried to kill him some years before. A protracted gun fight around the city's harbour follows, and Lee is wounded, losing part of an ear. But killing his man in return and now with the help of that great fighting bear Iorek Byrnison, another favourite character, he just escapes in his balloon, taking Iorek with him to pastures new.

This little book, the same size and format as *Lyra's Oxford*, contains more spoof newspaper cuttings and other examples of past printed ephemera. There is also a board game tucked in at the back with the title Peril of the Pole. Lovingly devised and clearly written as much for Pullman's own pleasure as anything else, it has no higher purpose than general entertainment. Two intriguing hand-written letters at the end of the book, written as if from Lyra, now a mature student, reveal that she is currently at St Sophia's College, Oxford, studying for a master's course in the history faculty.

The dissertation she has chosen is on: 'Development in patterns of trade in the European Arctic region with particular reference to independent cargo balloon carriage (1950–1970).' A newspaper cutting she refers to as one of her sources is included in the book on the previous page. It is a hugely biased account of the harbour fight, written the day after by the journalist Oskar Sigurdsson, still smarting from having been kicked into the sea by Lee Scoresby as punishment for his lying and dishonesty. Lee Scoresby, misspelled as Leigh Scroby, and his great bear companion in arms are also mentioned. So once again Lyra has managed to make contact, albeit at an academic distance, with two of her greatest friends and allies of before.

Of greater significance is the fact that Lyra, seen as a hard-working school girl in *Lyra's Oxford*, is now a successful college student with eventual plans to become a university teacher. She has therefore fulfilled the promise she made to herself and Will years ago to work hard and lead a productive life. She also refers to her continued quest to research into how her alethiometer works, reporting good progress here too. Any mention of Will would have been inappropriate in the two business-like letters from her reproduced here. But the energy and feeling of general engagement with life that comes across in them suggests that she is surviving well. For readers who have followed her turbulent life from a ten-year-old girl onwards, this final positive image of a busy, committed student makes for a pleasantly reassuring last word after the multitude of highs and lows that have taken place around her before.

Interview with Philip Pullman

Interview with Philip Pullman by Nicholas Tucker,
9 December 2016.

NICHOLAS TUCKER: It's some time since you wrote *His Dark Materials*. Do you often find yourself looking back to it now it is going to be newly televised by the BBC?

PHILIP PULLMAN: I do, constantly, because I am writing the successor to it, *The Book of Dust*, and I have to keep checking facts, like what was so and so's name and what sort of dæmon did they have. But also because I want to regain some of the energy I had when I was writing it. I well remember coming to the end of the first book and my normal practice had been to write three pages a day by hand on A4 narrow lined paper. But I was running out of money. I had almost got through my publisher's advance and things were getting a bit desperately tight. I was still working part-time at Westminster College, but I did have this sense of urgency. So I decided to up my output to five pages a day and what's more punish myself by not drinking any alcohol during the last hundred pages or whatever it was. It was a hot summer and I was in a state of suspended animation really. That was a period when I probably worked more intensely than any time before or since. But it was a good state to be in and I think about it now trying to get back to something like the same state 25 years later.

NT: Was there ever a moment when you felt the story started telling you?

PP: Yes, to an extent it did. There are things a story wants to do and there are things that you want to do. And in the end the story wins because it knows better than I do. There's an odd sense that one is discovering rather than inventing. There's a sense in which the story almost seems to be there in some Platonic realm and what I must do is try to transmit that pure sense to paper rather than go in for any clever stuff of my own. It's curious, because I don't actually believe in Platonic realms of pure being yet writing feels more like discovering rather than merely going along with a literary construct that's only made of words. So I do believe instinctively that it is in fact all out there somewhere and I am just writing it down. I can't justify that at all but there it is.

NT: Some of the epic scenes in *His Dark Materials* remind me of great opera. Do you ever write with music playing yourself?

PP: Never, never never. The reason is a simple one – it's to do with rhythm. I have to hear the rhythms of the sentences as I'm writing them. In fact I can hear the rhythm of the sentence I want to write next even before I know what words I've got to go with it. And if there is any music going on however distant it makes this almost impossible. That's why I had a shed built, because my oldest son was learning the violin. He was very good at it and became a professional musician. But I was listening to that rather than to my words. Other noises don't worry me a bit. Pneumatic drills, traffic, I can put up with all that. But music is an absolute killer. I love music. I listen to it a lot and play it as best I can on various instruments. But I never listen to it when I'm writing.

NT: Do you use different skills when you are editing what you have written?

PP: Yes. The sort of thing I deal with when editing might involve working on hastily written sentences where you can't quite tell who the 'he' or 'she' referred to actually is. Another little principle that I've found useful when I'm writing a scene is to make sure the reader gets some sense of where we are, indoors or outside. What the weather's like? Is it sunny? Is it raining? Who's present? Those things are important to me as a reader because I like to know them. They would certainly be important if this was also something that was going to appear on the screen since the script-writer, the director, the designer all need to know these things. So I always try to clarify what I am writing about with a little touch of things like that. Not overwhelming everything with detail but including just enough.

NT: So now your work has been televised and filmed, has the realisation that what you put down on paper might well in time appear on the screen changed the way you write?

PP: I genuinely don't think it has. I do write with the sense very far back in my consciousness that maybe what I'm doing may one day be adapted for something. But mainly it's the experience on the paper that I want to get right. I want to get back to the eye and the ear of the reader.

NT: When I say the name *Lyra* which particular image drawn from the subsequent play, film, or from the original story comes to mind?

PP: At the moment I am writing *The Book of Dust* which is also about Lyra, so the image that comes to mind at the moment is of someone who hasn't been seen yet and therefore hasn't been inhabited by another face or voice. So only I can see that face at the moment.

NT: What about Mrs Coulter? Is it possible to see any face now for her other than the one created so memorably by Nicole Kidman?

PP: She certainly did the part brilliantly. One extra reason I was sorry they didn't do the whole trilogy was because I wanted to see her change from being a cold-hearted, ideology-driven tyrant to someone who's feeling the love for Lyra is growing within her and her trying to push this feeling away. I wanted to see her do that change and I know she could have done it because she is a wonderful actress and could have made that whole transition look totally convincing.

NT: Did you always know that Mrs Coulter was going to come good in the end?

PP: It stole up on me rather than being a sudden revelation. I love Mrs Coulter dearly. I always treated her with the greatest, wary respect in all her scenes. She was ghastly really but also wonderful to write about. I'd run a mile from her in real life.

In the scene in the Himalayan Cave where she is hiding out with Lyra at the start of *The Amber Spyglass*, at one moment she pulls down a bat from the roof. She then gives this to her dæmon, who tears it apart. I saw that happen in real life at the zoo in the Burford Wildlife Park in a cage full of gibbons. These are very attractive creatures with long arms which they swing about with. A bird, I think a starling, flew down to pick up a crumb outside the enclosure. A long grey arm instantly shot out through the bars, dragging the bird squawking and flapping into the cage. The other gibbons came round to see what was going on while the poor bird itself was demolished. People started shouting, because the creature was obviously causing such extreme pain and misery to the bird. But what was it doing? This wasn't evil, it was just pure curiosity. But morally a very odd moment. And I used that when I had Mrs Coulter give the bat to her monkey dæmon.

NT: You have said recently that you are reading more William Blake. What are you finding there?

PP: Blake once wrote these words to his friend Thomas Butts:

> *Now I a fourfold vision see,*
> *And a fourfold vision is given to me:*
> *'Tis fourfold in my supreme delight*
> *And threefold in soft Beulah's night*
> *And twofold always, may God us keep*
> *From single vision and Newton's sleep!*

Now single vision in Newton's sleep is the sort of deadly scientific reductionism that says everything can be explained by the movement of impersonal particles. Twofold vision is when we see things as human beings do, viewing everything through a penumbra of memories, hopes, associations, and so on, reacting in an essentially human way. Threefold vision is what he meant by poetic inspiration and fourfold vision is what I think he meant by mystical ecstasy – a moment of intense identification with the natural world. And following Blake, I believe that all four ways of reacting can be used by a writer according to what they are trying to achieve at different moments.

NT: Have you ever got to fourfold vision yourself?

PP: Once when I was a boy, in a storm on the beach. And another time, when I was newly married, I remember coming home from my work as a library assistant going to our little flat in Barnes. And everything seemed to be double, everything seemed to have a parallel somewhere else. I remember seeing a group of people standing in a circle around a busker and the next thing I saw was a newspaper placard showing a picture of more people standing in a circle round a hijacked plane in Jordan somewhere. That sort of doubling I saw all the way. It was as if the whole universe was connected, leaving me in a state of gibbering excitement. Those were the only two times I have felt what Blake I think was referring to as fourfold vision. It is important never to rely entirely upon single vision. We must use all our faculties and senses always. Single vision is death.

NT: What about innocence? Should we always be in a hurry to leave this state behind us in order to work towards wisdom instead?

PP: I have never wanted to extirpate innocence. I don't want to thrust the facts of life on children of four or five. What I'm against in a quite visceral, loathing way, is the sentimental vision of childhood you get in books written in the so-called Golden Age of children's literature. Peter Pan, who thinks it's better always to stay a child, some of A.A. Milne's verses, I can't bear them, they make me sick! Children don't want to be children – they want to be grown up. The games they play are about being adult. Recalling my own adolescence, and encountering sexuality and intellectual excitement was all part of an extraordinary wonderful, glorious awakening. The whole universe began to sing. So when you get people like C.S. Lewis in the Narnia books lamenting the fact that children have to grow up it makes me very angry.

NT: What about religion? Have your own feelings about it changed over the last decade?

PP: Well in a way they have. When I was writing *The Good Man Jesus and the Scoundrel Christ* I read the gospels right through making lots of notes. And what struck me was how different the accounts were of Jesus according to who was telling the tale. That for some people makes the whole story more convincing because that divergence of views over what actually happened is exactly what you hear as members of a jury when witnesses are telling you what they thought they saw at the time. I see their point but I don't agree with it.

And if you look at all the other apocryphal gospel accounts, as the Biblical scholar as well as ghost story writer M.R. James once pointed out, you can see exactly why they were left out because they are bloody awful and don't work as stories. Matthew, Mark, Luke and John are easily the best told of the lot. And there are wonderful fictional moments within them. Who saw Satan coming to Jesus in the desert? No one did. It's obviously fiction. When Jesus was alone in the garden of Gethsemane when all the disciples were asleep, how do we know he said: 'My Father, if it is possible, let this cup pass me by.' It must have been an invention but it is also an extraordinary moment of imaginative and emotional power. When you look at the four gospels as a storyteller, you can see exactly how well they work.

So I think a bit more subtly now about the Christian story. I can't also deny how good some religious people are. They set about doing good a lot of the time for reasons I don't believe in but which are satisfactory for them. I have always felt that a measure of goodness is not what you believe but what you do. And religion can supply a sense of community to some people. I once put this to Richard Dawkins: if you had a little girl who was terribly ill and knew she was soon going to die, do you tell her the stark facts of her oncoming death?

Of course you don't! You tell her a fairy tale about going to heaven. What else can you possibly do?

NT: So when did you start doubting the Christianity that you had been brought up in?

PP: I think the first thing I read that made me start thinking in a contrary way was Colin Wilson's once famous book *The Outsider*. And that pointed me at people like Nietzsche and Kierkegaard and got me thinking in a new way. After that I got interested in existentialism and all that stuff and poor old God just got shuffled away. I floated in and out of various other beliefs in my twenties. I was a Buddhist for a bit and then got interested in the occult and astrology. But they all fell away. I still remain very interested in the esoteric but not as a believer. But people like Dawkins, who dismiss religion entirely as utter foolishness, I think are simply wrong.

NT: *His Dark Materials* starts with a child who by the end is turning into a newly sexualised young adult. This is in contrast to many other children's books where characters often seem to stay the same age from start to finish.

PP: That's one of the main themes of the whole trilogy. When Lyra and Will kiss for the first time they don't have to do anything more than kiss. But if you can't remember what your first kiss was like I feel sorry for you.

NT: Broadly speaking almost all children's and young adult novels have endings that if not always entirely happy at least make moral sense. Do you feel this applies to *His Dark Materials* too?

PP: Well, such endings happen more frequently than we might think with adult books too. She marries him; the murder is solved or whatever. Books that are popular and read and talked about usually have endings that actually satisfy in a moral sense whether they are happy or not. The ending of *His Dark Materials* made lots of people cry – it made me cry too. But it was also satisfying, I hope, because it didn't offer easy options after so much that had gone before.